SOLO JOURNEY

90 Days to discovering the Woman God Created You to Be

DR. RITA CARTER

SOLO JOURNEY

90 Days to discovering the Woman God Created You to Be

HOV Publishing is a division of HOV, LLC.
www.hovpub.com
email: hopeofvision@gmail.com

Editing & Proofreading: HOV Publishing Editorial Team
Front Cover Design and Inside layout by HOV Design Solutions

To learn more about Dr. Rita's coaching and speaking services or to schedule a free discovery call, please visit her website at www.breakthroughready.com

Social Media:
Facebook: https://www.facebook.com/BreakthroughwithRita
Instagram: https://www.instagram.com/breakthroughwithrita/

ISBN Paperback: 978-1-955107-26-6
ISBN eBook: 978-1-955107-25-9

Printed in the United States of America

Dedication

To the woman on her journey—

This is for you.

For the woman who has carried burdens too heavy for her shoulders yet continues to rise each day with quiet strength. For the woman who has smiled when her heart was breaking, who has given more than she had, and who has questioned if there was still more to her story.

This journey is for the woman who knows deep within that she was created for more, that God has called her, chosen her, and set her apart for such a time as this (Esther 4:14). It is for the woman who is tired of merely surviving and is ready to live fully, freely, and authentically in the presence of God.

As you step into these pages, may you feel a holy stirring within a burning desire not just to change, but to be transformed. May the words you read remind you that you are seen, known, and loved by the God who shaped the heavens and still calls you, His daughter.

This devotional is more than reflection; it is a journey toward freedom. It is a call to lay down what no longer serves you, to rise above what tried to break you, and to boldly step into the radiant woman God created you to be.

To you, this is my prayer: that your *solo journey* would awaken courage, ignite faith, and unlock destiny.

With all my heart,
Dr. Rita Carter

A Blessing for the Journey

Beautiful, may you rise each morning clothed in strength and dignity (Proverbs 31:25).
May your weary heart find rest in the arms of the One who never leaves you (Matthew 11:28).
May courage be your companion, hope your anchor, and love your constant song.

As you walk this path, may every step draw you nearer to your true self in Christ.
May you release the weight of yesterday and embrace the promise of tomorrow.
And may you come to know, beyond all doubt, that you are chosen, called, and deeply loved.

In Jesus' Name, Amen.

Preface

"Thus says the Lord: 'Stand at the crossroads and look; ask for the ancient paths, ask where the good way is, and walk in it, and you will find rest for your souls.'" — Jeremiah 6:16

This is the journey within.

Not a journey of miles, but of moments.

Not a journey of crowds, but of stillness.

Not a journey of answers, but of surrender.

Every solo journey begins with a crossroads. Perhaps you are here because life has shifted, loss has visited, or you simply feel the tug of something greater within you. Whatever the reason, God has drawn you to this place of pause, this holy invitation to walk with Him into deeper waters.

A solo journey is not about isolation but transformation. Jesus Himself often withdrew to lonely places to pray (Luke 5:16). He knew that solitude was the soil where strength was renewed and clarity was born. Likewise, your time in this journey is not wasted; it is sacred ground, a season where God whispers identity, heals old wounds, and reminds you of His unfailing love.

As you step into these pages, remember: God walks before you (Deuteronomy 31:8), surrounds you with His presence (Psalm 139:5), and promises to complete the good work He began in you (Philippians 1:6). You are not merely reading words; you are stepping into a divine appointment.

Day 1:

The First Step

Scripture:

"Forget the former things; do not dwell on the past. See, I am doing a new thing! Now it springs up; do you not perceive it?"—Isaiah 43:18–19 (NIV)

Devotional Reflection:

Every significant transformation begins with a single, deliberate step, often a quiet one, unseen by others but deeply felt within. That first step is sacred. It's where courage speaks louder than fear and where hope stretches further than history.

You may be stepping into this journey unsure of what you'll discover or afraid of what you'll have to confront. Maybe you're grieving who you thought you were supposed to be, or you're exhausted from carrying roles and expectations that were never meant for you. Maybe you're waking up to the realization that you've built a life that looks good on the outside but feels misaligned within.

God is inviting you to pause and hear Him say, *"Daughter, I am doing something new in you."* That "new thing" may not look like a grand announcement or dramatic change. It may start with a whisper in your spirit, a longing for more, or a quiet stirring that says, *"I don't want to keep living like this."*

This solo journey is not about running from the world, it's about running toward the truth. The truth of who you are beneath the masks, beneath the wounds, beneath the performing and pretending. It's about discovering the voice that's been silenced by others' opinions and awakening the dreams that were buried beneath years of self-doubt.

This is a shedding season. A sacred unraveling. And yes, it may feel uncomfortable. But growth often begins where comfort ends. God is not calling you to a path of perfection, but a path of *presence*; His and yours.

This first step is not about having all the answers. It's about being willing to ask the right questions. It's about choosing to believe that you are worthy of healing, worthy of peace, and worthy of discovering the woman you were always meant to be. The one who existed before the heartbreak, before the labels, before life told you who you had to become in order to survive.

God is not just waiting at the finish line; He's walking with you through every mile of this journey. Trust Him. The woman you are becoming is already within you. She's just been waiting for permission to rise.

Journey Prompts:

1. What emotions rise up when you think about walking this journey alone? Be honest, what excites you, and what scares you?

 ____
 ____
 ____
 ____

2. What roles, expectations, or versions of yourself have you outgrown but are still clinging to?

3. In what area of your life do you sense God whispering, *"I'm doing a new thing"?* What might that "new thing" look like?

Prayer:

Lord, I'm standing at the edge of something unfamiliar but necessary. Help me release the weight of my past and the fear of my future. Walk with me as I take this first step. Teach me to trust Your presence more than I fear the unknown. Let this journey begin with faith, not perfection. I want to find the woman You created me to be. In Jesus' Name, Amen.

Journal Notes:

Day 2:

Alone, But Not Abandoned

Scripture:

"Be strong and courageous. Do not be afraid or terrified because of them, for the Lord your God goes with you; He will never leave you nor forsake you."
—Deuteronomy 31:6 (NIV)

Devotional Reflection:

There is a difference between solitude and loneliness. One is a place of growth, clarity, and restoration. The other is a space of isolation, fear, and emptiness. Sometimes the line between them feels razor-thin, especially when you're stepping away from people, patterns, or places that used to give you a false sense of identity.

You may find yourself wondering, *"Am I making a mistake? Will I end up all alone?"* Those are valid fears. After all, we were created for connection. But there's something sacred about learning to walk alone with God, not because you've been abandoned, but because He's calling you to discover His voice without the noise of others.

In this season, you might not be surrounded by applause or affirmation. You might not have people who understand the depth of your decision to discover yourself. That's okay.

You're not walking in circles; you're walking *into alignment*. Sometimes, God clears the room so He can speak directly to you.

This is your wilderness moment. But the wilderness is not a punishment; it's preparation. It's the place where God strips away the distractions, reveals your true identity, and teaches you how to trust Him in ways you never have before. Remember: even Jesus went into the wilderness *before* He stepped into His assignment.

So today, rest in the truth that you are never truly alone. The One who formed you walks beside you, speaks to you, and covers you. You are seen. You are held. You are guided, even here.

Journey Prompts:

1. In what ways do you confuse being alone with being unloved or unworthy?

   ____
   ____
   ____
   ____
   ____
   ____

2. How has God shown up for you in past seasons when you felt most isolated?

   ____
   ____
   ____
   ____
   ____

3. What might God be trying to show you in this quiet, in-between space?

Prayer:

Father, teach me to embrace this season of solitude with a spirit of trust, not fear. When the silence feels loud and the path feels lonely, remind me that You are right here. Help me release the need for outside validation and cling to Your presence. Shape me in the quiet. Anchor me in Your love. And let me grow in the stillness. In Jesus' Name, Amen.

Journal Notes:

Journal Notes:

Day 3:

Who Told You That?

Scripture:

"But the Lord God called to the man, 'Where are you?' He answered, "I heard You in the garden, and I was afraid because I was naked; so, I hid." And He said, "Who told you that you were naked?"—Genesis 3:9–11 (NIV)

Devotional Reflection:

Shame has a voice. And for too many of us, it's the loudest one we hear.

From an early age, most women are handed labels, by culture, by caretakers, by broken people doing the best they can. *Too loud. Too quiet. Too emotional. Not enough. Too much.* And over time, these words bury themselves into our identity until we can't tell where they end and we begin.

But today, God is asking the same question He asked Adam and Eve in the garden: *"Who told you that?"*

Who told you you're unworthy of love?
Who told you your past disqualifies your future?
Who told you your voice doesn't matter, or that your dreams are too late?

Sometimes, we inherit beliefs that didn't begin with us, but if we don't confront them, they *will* end with us.

God's question wasn't about their nakedness, it was about their *awareness*. For the first time, Adam and Eve saw themselves through the eyes of shame, not the eyes of love. And shame will always lead us to hide. But God isn't afraid of what's exposed; He's after what's hidden. Because in our hiding, we begin to believe we're unworthy of being fully seen.

One woman who had to confront shame and step into wholeness was the woman at the well (John 4). Rejected by her community and ashamed of her past, she came to the well at a time when no one else would be there. But Jesus *met her there*. Not to condemn her, but to tell her that He saw her, knew her story, and still offered her *living water*, a new identity and a new beginning.

Today, God is calling you to unlearn what shame taught you. To replace those false labels with His truth. To stop hiding and start healing.

Journey Prompts:

1. What false beliefs about yourself have you been carrying that no longer serve you? Where did they come from?

   ____
   ____
   ____
   ____
   ____
   ____

2. When you think about your identity, is it based more on people's opinions or God's truth?

____
____
____
____
____
____

3. What do you hear God saying to your heart today about who you truly are?

____
____
____
____
____
____

Prayer:

Lord, open my ears to hear *Your truth* louder than every lie I've believed. Silence the voices of shame, doubt, and fear. Reveal the places where I've been hiding out of insecurity. Teach me how to see myself the way You see me, redeemed, loved, and worthy of every promise You've made. Today, I reject the lies and choose to walk in the truth. In Jesus' Name, Amen.

Journal Notes:

Day 4:

When the Mirror Lies

Scripture:

"For now we see only a reflection as in a mirror; then we shall see face to face. Now I know in part; then I shall know fully, even as I am fully known."—1 Corinthians 13:12 (NIV)

Devotional Reflection:

What do you see when you look in the mirror?

Not just the physical reflection, but the woman behind the eyes. The one who's loved and lost. The one who's survived things no one else knows about. The one who smiles out of habit but cries when no one's watching.

So many of us have learned to mistrust our own reflection, not because it isn't true, but because the lens we're looking through is cracked. Distorted by comparison. Fogged by rejection. Shaped by a lifetime of being measured by what we produce, how we perform, or how we're perceived.

But the mirror lies when it's not aligned with God's view of you.

You are *not* what happened to you.
You are *not* your body.

You are *not* the sum of others' expectations.
You are *not* too late, too old, or too far gone.

Your identity is not defined by what the world sees, but by what God knows. And He sees all of you: the hidden pain, the buried dreams, the secret prayers, and still calls you *"beloved."*

Consider Hannah in 1 Samuel. To others, she may have looked like a barren, broken woman begging for something she'd never have. But God saw a mother. A vessel of legacy. A woman of faith so fierce that her prayers became history. The world labeled her barren. God called her chosen.

What if your reflection could reflect *that* truth? What if, instead of seeing what's missing, you started seeing what's *becoming*?

You don't need another filter. You need freedom. And it starts by seeing yourself through the eyes of the One who made you.

Journey Prompts:

1. When you look at yourself, what parts of your identity feel distorted or unclear?

   ____

   ____

   ____

   ____

   ____

   ____

2. What labels have you internalized that don't reflect who you truly are?

   ____

   ____

3. What would it look like to see yourself the way God sees you; fully known, fully loved?

Prayer:

Father, help me see beyond the surface. Heal the places in me that reject Your truth. When I doubt my worth, remind me that I was formed by Your hands and called by Your name. Strip away every false label and broken lens that clouds my identity. Let my reflection align with Your truth and let me walk in it with confidence. In Jesus' Name, Amen.

Journal Notes:

Journal Notes:

Day 5:

Permission to Change

Scripture:

"Do not conform to the pattern of this world, but be transformed by the renewing of your mind. Then you will be able to test and approve what God's will is—His good, pleasing and perfect will."—Romans 12:2 (NIV)

Devotional Reflection:

One of the hardest things to do is change in front of people who only know the older version of you. You might be ready to grow, but they still expect you to stay the same. You might be stepping into healing, but they're more comfortable with your brokenness.

But here's the truth, you don't need anyone else's permission to evolve. God already gave you His.

Sometimes the people around you are more committed to your past than your future. Not because they're malicious, but because your transformation threatens the version of you that made them comfortable. But this journey isn't about keeping others comfortable, it's about being faithful to the woman God is shaping you to be.

Lot's wife (Genesis 19) was given a clear path to freedom, but she turned around. Why? Because the awareness of what was behind her felt safer than the unknown future ahead. She longed for a version of life she had outgrown. And in doing so, she became stuck, literally and spiritually.

Don't let that be your story.

The Apostle Paul reminds us in Philippians 3:13–14: "Forgetting what is behind and straining toward what is ahead, I press on toward the goal to win the prize for which God has called me heavenward in Christ Jesus." This means releasing the grip of what was, past mistakes, old labels, former relationships, and leaning into the new thing God is doing in you.

There is grace for your process. There is beauty in your becoming. You're allowed to change your mind, your habits, your boundaries, your relationships, and your pace. You're allowed to heal differently than others expected. You're allowed to rise, even if it confuses the ones who knew you during your fall.

And yes, it may be lonely at first. Growth often creates a gap between where you were and where you're going. But remember, that gap isn't empty, it's where God meets you, shapes you, and strengthens you for the next season.

Transformation isn't about perfection, it's about alignment. It's when your heart, your habits, and your hope begin to reflect who you truly are in Christ.

You are not obligated to remain who pain created. You are free to become who God designed. And when you fully embrace that freedom, you'll stop asking, "Who will be okay with my change?" and start declaring, "Lord, I'm okay with who You are making me to be."

Journey Prompts:

1. Where in your life are you craving change but afraid of how others will respond?

   ____
   ____
   ____
   ____
   ____
   ____

2. What version of yourself are you ready to release in order to make room for growth?

   ____
   ____
   ____
   ____
   ____
   ____

3. What does "renewing your mind" look like for you in this season of transformation?

   ____
   ____
   ____
   ____
   ____
   ____

Prayer:

Lord, I no longer want to live trapped in who I used to be. Give me the strength to evolve, even when it feels uncomfortable. Help me let go of what I've outgrown, thoughts, people, patterns, and walk boldly into the woman You're shaping me to be. I give myself permission to change, and I trust You with the outcome. In Jesus' Name, Amen.

Journal Notes:

Journal Notes:

Day 6:

The Whisper of God

Scripture:

"Be silent before the Sovereign Lord, for the day of the Lord is near."— Zephaniah 1:7 (NIV)

Devotional Reflection:

Today's society glorifies hustle, noise, and constant connection, silence can feel like a punishment. But what if silence is not a void, but a vessel?

Sometimes, God does His deepest work in quiet places.

Maybe you've noticed that certain people are no longer calling. The invitations have slowed down. The distractions that used to numb the pain are no longer satisfying. It feels like everything is... still. Unsettlingly still.

But don't mistake divine stillness for divine absence.

God often speaks the loudest in moments when everything else goes quiet. It's in the hush of solitude that your soul begins to exhale, your mind begins to detox, and your heart becomes available for truth. The silence is not here to harm you. It's here to heal you.

The prophet Elijah knew this well. After calling down fire from heaven, he ran into the wilderness; tired, afraid, and overwhelmed. He expected God to show up in dramatic ways: wind, fire, and earthquakes. But instead, the Lord whispered in a gentle breeze (1 Kings 19:11–12). Sometimes the breakthrough isn't in the noise, but in the whisper.

The truth is that silence has a ministry of its own. It strips away the false comforts, unmasks the distractions, and invites you into the kind of intimacy with God that constant noise could never allow. It's in the quiet that He tends to wounds you didn't even know you had, prunes away what can't stay in your next season, and strengthens you for what's ahead.

We tend to fear what we cannot control, and silence is one of those things. We can control what we say, but we can't control what God will reveal when we get quiet enough to listen. That's why silence is sacred, it's where surrender begins.

David understood this when he wrote, "Truly my soul finds rest in God; my salvation comes from him" (Psalm 62:1). Rest isn't just physical, it's spiritual. Silence is the soil where trust grows.

So, what if this season of stillness is God's preparation for your next assignment? What if the doors you've been praying for won't open until you've allowed the quiet to do its work?

The silence is God making space. For your clarity. For your healing. For your voice to rise again, unfiltered by the world's expectations.

What if this silence isn't something to escape, but something to embrace?

Journey Prompts:

1. How do you typically respond to silence, do you fill it, avoid it, or lean into it? Why?

    ____
    ____
    ____
    ____
    ____
    ____

2. What has God been trying to reveal to you in this quieter season of your life?

    ____
    ____
    ____
    ____
    ____
    ____

3. How can you create intentional space in your day to simply *be still* and listen?

    ____
    ____
    ____
    ____
    ____
    ____

Prayer:

Father, teach me not to fear the quiet. Help me see silence as sacred, not empty. Strip away the noise that drowns out Your voice. Let me feel Your presence even in the stillness. Whisper truth to my weary places and remind me that even in the silence, You are near. In Jesus' Name, Amen.

Journal Notes:

Journal Notes:

Day 7: When the Walls Fall Down

Scripture:

"He heals the brokenhearted and binds up their wounds."
—Psalm 147:3 (NIV)

Devotional Reflection:

Some of the strongest women you know are the ones who've mastered the art of building walls.

Walls that say, *"I'm fine."*
Walls that say, *"I don't need anyone."*
Walls that were born out of betrayal, abandonment, disappointment, and loss.

And truthfully? Those walls may have protected you for a time. They kept your heart from shattering further. They helped you survive when you didn't know how to heal. But now, those same walls that kept pain out are also keeping *God* out. And love. And peace. And freedom.

At some point, surviving is no longer enough. You were created to *thrive*.

But thriving requires vulnerability. And vulnerability requires trust.

Think of Ruth, who chose to walk away from everything familiar to follow Naomi into a land she didn't know, to a future she couldn't see. She had every reason to build walls, she was widowed, displaced, and uncertain. But instead of hiding behind grief, she opened her heart to possibility. And in doing so, she stepped into destiny.

God is not intimidated by the walls you've built. But He *is* inviting you to let Him tear them down, gently, intentionally, and lovingly. Not to leave you exposed, but to heal what's been hidden.

You don't have to be the strong one all the time. You don't have to keep pretending you're okay. Real strength is found in surrender. And the only way to truly move forward is to stop hiding behind what once protected you.

Healing begins when the walls fall down.

Journey Prompts:

1. What emotional walls have you built to protect yourself from further pain?

   ____
   ____
   ____
   ____
   ____
   ____

2. How are those walls helping you and how are they hindering you?

   ____
   ____

3. What would it look like to invite God into the places you've kept guarded for so long?

Prayer:

Lord, I've learned how to protect myself, but now I want to learn how to *heal*. I don't want to live behind walls anymore. I invite You into the guarded places of my heart. Help me release the fear of being seen and soften what's been hardened by life. Let Your love be the shelter I trust. Heal what I thought I had to hide. In Jesus' Name, Amen.

Journal Notes:

Journal Notes:

Day 8:

Learning to Trust Again

Scripture:

"Trust in the Lord with all your heart and lean not on your own understanding; in all your ways submit to Him, and He will make your paths straight."—Proverbs 3:5–6 (NIV)

Devotional Reflection:

Trust doesn't come easily when your heart has been broken. It's even harder when the person you're trying to trust… is *you*.

When life has handed you betrayal, abandonment, or failure, trust begins to feel like a gamble. So instead, we become self-reliant. We try to predict, plan, and protect ourselves from future disappointment. And slowly, without realizing it, we stop trusting others, stop trusting God and worst of all, we stop trusting *ourselves*.

You may be wrestling with thoughts like:
"How did I let that happen?"
"Why didn't I see the signs?"
"What if I choose wrong again?"

But what if you could extend grace to yourself the way God already has?

God never asked you to know everything. He asked you to trust Him with everything, even the parts you don't understand. Even the version of yourself that made choices from a place of pain or fear. Even the mistakes that you've been punishing yourself for in silence.

Consider Sarah, the wife of Abraham. She doubted God's promise, tried to control the outcome, and even laughed at the idea that she could still conceive. And yet, despite her detour and disbelief, God *still fulfilled His word.* Her failure to trust perfectly did not cancel her destiny.

The same is true for you. Your past does not disqualify your future. God doesn't need your perfection; He simply needs your *permission* to work through your surrender.

This is your season to try again. To believe again. To trust again. Not just in others, but in God's voice within you.

Journey Prompts:

1. What past experience caused you to stop trusting God, others, or yourself?

 ____

 ____

 ____

 ____

 ____

 ____

2. In what areas of your life are you still trying to control the outcome out of fear?

 ____

 ____

3. What would it feel like to fully surrender your plans and emotions to God, even if you don't understand everything yet?

Prayer:

Father, I want to trust again but sometimes fear feels louder than faith. Heal the parts of me that are still bracing for disappointment. Teach me to trust You even when I don't have the full picture. Help me forgive myself for what I didn't know then. Lead me step by step, and help me believe that You are faithful, even when I've fallen short. In Jesus' Name, Amen.

Journal Notes:

Journal Notes:

Day 9:

Starting Over Isn't Failing

Scripture:

"Because of the Lord's great love we are not consumed, for His compassions never fail. They are new every morning; great is Your faithfulness."—Lamentations 3:22–23 (NIV)

Devotional Reflection:

There's something humbling about starting over. Whether it's leaving a relationship, changing careers, rebuilding after a mistake, or returning to yourself after years of pretending, starting over feels like both an ending and a beginning.

But let this truth anchor you today: starting over isn't failing. In fact, it takes more courage to begin again than it does to stay stuck in something that's no longer serving you.

God specializes in new beginnings. His mercies are new every morning, not just once, not just on birthdays, not just on January 1st, but every single day. He's not holding your past over your head; He's holding the door open for your future.

Starting over might feel like you're behind. But in God's timing, you're right on schedule.

Take Naomi, for example. After the death of her husband and sons, she returned to Bethlehem empty, bitter, and grieving. She even tried to rename herself "Mara," meaning "bitter." Yet, in that place of sorrow, God birthed something new, not just in Naomi, but through Ruth, whose obedience and faith brought about the lineage of Jesus Himself. Naomi's story didn't end in bitterness; it bloomed into legacy.

And then there's Peter. The disciple who swore he'd never deny Jesus... and then did it three times in one night. That failure could have been the end of his ministry. Shame could have swallowed him whole. But Jesus met him on the shore after the resurrection, restored him with love, and sent him out to build the Church. Peter didn't just start over, he started stronger, with a testimony that would change the world.

Starting over isn't a detour; it's a declaration:
"I am no longer afraid to grow."
"I believe God still has more for me."
"I trust that what's ahead is worth rebuilding for."

You are not back at square one. You are starting again with wisdom, resilience, and the presence of God.

Sometimes starting over means letting go of what almost worked to embrace what God has actually prepared. It's not about erasing your past; it's about allowing God to redeem it. Every ending in Him is simply a doorway to a new chapter filled with grace, purpose, and hope.

So, lift your head. Wipe your tears. Take the first step forward. This is not the end of your story, it's the beginning of a better one.

Journey Prompts:

1. What situation or area of your life feels like it's forcing you to start over?

   ____
   ____
   ____
   ____
   ____
   ____

2. What fears or beliefs are keeping you from fully embracing a new beginning?

   ____
   ____
   ____
   ____
   ____
   ____

3. What lesson or strength are you bringing with you into this new chapter?

   ____
   ____
   ____
   ____
   ____
   ____

Prayer:

God, I release the fear that starting over means I've failed. Thank You for Your endless mercy and Your ability to make all things new, even me. Remind me that every ending is also a beginning, and You are with me through each step. Give me boldness to begin again, and faith to believe that this new chapter will be better than the last. In Jesus' Name, Amen.

Journal Notes:

Journal Notes:

Day 10:

Your Scars Still Shine

Scripture:

"But He was pierced for our transgressions, He was crushed for our iniquities; the punishment that brought us peace was on Him, and by His wounds we are healed."

—Isaiah 53:5 (NIV)

Devotional Reflection:

Scars are complicated. Some fade without a trace. Others linger, etched into our skin, our minds, and our memories. They carry both the residue of what broke us and the brilliance of what couldn't destroy us.

Many of us were taught to hide our scars, to wear makeup over the bruises, to smile over the sadness, to keep moving as if nothing happened. And yet, in God's hands, the places where we've bled become the very places where He brings breakthrough.

Some scars tell of survival. Others of surrender. But all of them tell of grace.

Think back to the moments you've walked through fire, maybe silently. Maybe alone. Maybe in full view of the world. You've endured rejection, abandonment, betrayal, heartbreak, disappointment. And while others may have only seen the surface, God saw every hidden wound. He saw you bleeding in places no one else could see.

Here's the holy truth: your scars shine. They shine with the light of redemption. They shine with the glow of healing. They shine because they are no longer wounds, they are witnesses.

Jesus Himself knows the ministry of scars. After His resurrection, He didn't hide His wounds, He showed them to His disciples. Those nail prints weren't marks of defeat; they were proof of victory. Proof that the grave couldn't hold Him. Proof that love overcame death. Your scars serve that same purpose to remind you (and others) that the worst thing you've been through didn't win.

Think of the woman with the issue of blood. For 12 years, she bled. She suffered in silence. She spent everything she had trying to get better. But when she reached for Jesus, He didn't just stop the bleeding, He restored her identity. She went from being "unclean" to being called "daughter." Her story, and perhaps the scars that remained became a testimony still spoken about thousands of years later.

Your scars may be emotional, physical, or spiritual. You may wish they'd disappear. But they carry a unique anointing, evidence that the enemy lost, that God was faithful, and that you lived.

And here's the part the enemy doesn't want you to know: your scars don't just mark where you've been, they light the way for someone else's healing. When you show them, you're saying, "I've been there, and God brought me through. And if He did it for me, He can do it for you."

So don't be ashamed of the marks you carry. You are not just a woman who made it, you are a woman marked by God. And baby girl, that shine? It's not from pain. It's from purpose.

Journey Prompts:

1. What physical, emotional, or spiritual scars do you carry that still feel unresolved?

   ____

   ____

   ____

2. What have your scars taught you about God's faithfulness and your resilience?

   ____

   ____

   ____

3. How might your story and your scars help someone else feel less alone?

   ____

   ____

   ____

Prayer:

Lord, help me to see my scars not as signs of shame, but as reminders of Your healing. I thank You for every moment You carried me through pain. Let my story be a light for others who are still in the dark. I trust that nothing I've been through will be wasted in Your hands. In Jesus' Name, Amen.

Journal Notes:

Day 11:

When You Feel Behind

Scripture:

"So, the last will be first, and the first will be last."
—Matthew 20:16 (NIV)

Devotional Reflection:

We live in a time that moves fast, scrolling, streaming, posting, and pressuring. It's no wonder so many of us feel like we're constantly trying to catch up to a version of life we *think* we should be living by now.

You look around and see people seemingly miles ahead, married, successful, traveling, launching businesses, securing speaking engagements, building dream homes. And then there's you... feeling like you're just trying to get out of bed and hold on to hope.

The enemy loves to use comparisons to distort your vision and attack your value. He plants lies like:
"You should be further along."
"Look how far they are."
"You're too old now."
"You missed your moment."

But the enemy doesn't know the end of your story; *God does.*

God does not operate by your watch. He doesn’t panic over deadlines. He doesn't need your pace to match the world’s speed. He’s doing something deeper *within you* that can’t be rushed. Something rooted. Something eternal.

Take heart in the stories of women who bloomed late, Sarah, Elizabeth, Naomi. They weren’t forgotten. They were *being prepared* for a divine reveal.

God isn’t withholding anything from you; He’s reserving something *for* you.

When you feel behind, remember delay does not mean denial. God is still writing your story, and He does *His best work* in the waiting.

Journey Prompts:

1. In what area of life do you feel like you’re “falling behind”?

    ____
    ____
    ____
    ____
    ____
    ____

2. Whose timeline are you measuring your progress against?

    ____
    ____
    ____
    ____
    ____
    ____

3. How can you begin to trust God's perfect timing for your journey?

Prayer:

Father, help me release the pressure to “keep up.” Silence the voice of comparison and let me rest in Your timing. I believe that what You have for me is still on the way. Let me embrace where I am today with gratitude and trust. In Jesus’ Name, Amen.

Journal Notes:

Journal Notes:

Day 12:

You are not here to please people

Scripture:

"Am I now trying to win the approval of human beings, or of God? Or am I trying to please people? If I were still trying to please people, I would not be a servant of Christ."
—Galatians 1:10 (NIV)

Devotional Reflection:

Saying "no" can feel like a betrayal when you've been conditioned to always be agreeable, available, and accommodating. You may wrestle with guilt, with fear, or with anxiety. You may worry that others will see you as selfish, difficult, or less "spiritual."

But hear this truth: "No" is not rejection; it's *direction.*

Your "no" is sacred. It's a shield. It's a boundary that honors the emotional, mental, and spiritual capacity God gave you.

Jesus Himself was the embodiment of love, but He wasn't afraid to disappoint human expectations. He withdrew from crowds when He was tired. He said "no" to certain demands so He could say "yes" to the Father's will. He refused to let the pressure of people override the purpose of God.

And yet, we often feel guilty about doing the same.

Many of us carry the weight of overcommitment because we've tied our worth to our *usefulness*. But being stretched thin doesn't make you more spiritual, it makes you *burnt out*.

Saying "no" creates margin. Margin for rest. Margin for joy. Margin for presence. It clears space for God to move, speak, and restore. And when you say "no" with clarity and kindness, you teach others that your life has boundaries and your soul has value.

You are not here to please people. You are here to *please God*. And sometimes, that means courageously declining what looks good in order to protect what *is* good, your peace.

Journey Prompts:

1. Where in your life have you been saying "yes" out of guilt, fear, or habit?

   ____
   ____
   ____
   ____
   ____
   ____

2. What boundary needs to be established or reinforced in this season?

   ____
   ____
   ____
   ____
   ____
   ____

3. How can you begin to see "no" as a path to freedom, not failure?

____
____
____
____
____
____

Prayer:

God, give me the courage to honor my limits. Teach me that "no" is not rejection, it's redirection. Help me create boundaries that protect my peace and preserve my purpose. Let every yes, I give be intentional, not automatic. In Jesus' Name, Amen.

Journal Notes:

____
____
____
____
____
____
____
____
____
____
____
____

Journal Notes:

Day 13:

Choosing Joy in the Journey

Scripture:

"The joy of the Lord is your strength."—Nehemiah 8:10 (NIV)

Devotional Reflection:

Joy can feel like a rebellious act when everything around you feels heavy. It's not the same as happiness, which is circumstantial. Happiness changes when the paycheck comes or when the relationship works out. But joy? Joy is deeper. It's anchored. It's spiritual. It lives in the bones of those who've seen pain, faced storms, and still choose to dance in the rain.

When life disappoints, joy is often the first thing to disappear. It gets buried under grief, under routine, under busyness, under the weight of what you thought life would be. But joy isn't just an emotion, it's a weapon. It's one of the ways you fight back against despair.

Joy says: I know Who I belong to.
Joy says: Even here, God is good.
Joy says: I don't have to have it all figured out to have peace in my heart.

Mary Magdalene's joy didn't come after everything was perfect. It came when she realized Jesus was alive when hope broke through the tomb. She knew darkness, demons, and rejection. But the light of joy found her in the garden of her grief. She became the first voice to proclaim resurrection. That's the power of joy, it turns graveyards into gardens, sorrow into strength, and endings into brand-new beginnings.

The Apostle Paul understood this, too. Sitting in a prison cell, he wrote to the Philippians about rejoicing, again and again. He didn't write about joy from a beach or a banquet table; he wrote it from a place of chains. That tells us joy is not about where we are, it's about Who is with us.

You don't have to wait until the breakthrough to feel joy. Joy is the breakthrough. Even if it's quiet. Even if it's small. Let it rise.

And sometimes joy isn't loud, it's steady. It's the smile you give even when tears are still drying. It's the peace that lets you sleep when the answers haven't come. It's the hope that whispers, God's not done yet.

Choosing joy doesn't mean ignoring pain, it means refusing to let pain have the final say. It's declaring that the same God who met you in the valley will walk with you to the mountaintop. It's knowing that joy isn't just a feeling, it's the fuel that keeps you going.

So, today, don't just wish for joy, choose it. Let it be your strength, your testimony, and your reminder that even in the middle of the journey, God is still writing a beautiful story.

Journey Prompts:

1. What's robbing you of joy right now? Be honest.

____
____
____
____
____
____

2. What small practices or moments have brought you joy in the past?

____
____
____
____
____
____

3. How can you begin to intentionally pursue joy in your current season?

____
____
____
____
____
____

Prayer:

Lord, I choose joy, even here, even now. Let joy be my strength, my anchor, and my light. When life feels heavy, help me remember that Your joy is not based on circumstances, it's based on Your unchanging presence. Let joy rise within me, unshaken. In Jesus' Name, Amen.

Journal Notes:

Journal Notes:

Day 14:

Becoming Her

Scripture:

"And we all... who with unveiled faces contemplate the Lord's glory, are being transformed into his image with ever-increasing glory, which comes from the Lord, who is the Spirit."—2 Corinthians 3:18 (NIV)

Devotional Reflection:

Becoming *her* isn't about reaching perfection, it's about returning to the truth of who God always knew you were.

She's not just a dream version of yourself. She's not a filtered Instagram fantasy. She's the woman who wakes up with grace in her bones and fire in her soul. She's the healed version. The whole version. The brave version. The *free* version.

But becoming her takes surrender. It takes intentional unlearning. It takes choosing *growth over comfort* every single day.

Maybe for years, you played small. You made yourself easy to digest. You performed. You blended in. But something inside you is rising now. A stirring. A knowing. A whisper from heaven saying, "There's more in you."

Becoming her means leaving behind the lies. It means showing up for yourself, not just when it's easy, but when it's *necessary.* It means letting God touch the places you've numbed, denied, or overlooked.

And here's the beauty: she's not far away. She's within you. You've seen glimpses of her. In the mirror. In your prayers. In your tears. She's been waiting.

God is calling you *into alignment*; mind, body, and spirit with who He created you to be before the trauma, before the labels, before the shame.

You are not just on a solo journey; you are *reintroducing yourself to yourself.* And that, dear one, is holy.

Journey Prompts:

1. Who is the woman you are becoming? Describe her in detail.

   ____
   ____
   ____
   ____
   ____
   ____

2. What habits, beliefs, or relationships are helping or hindering your transformation?

   ____
   ____
   ____
   ____
   ____
   ____

3. How will you honor the version of yourself that is emerging?

   ____

Prayer:

God, thank You for reminding me of who I truly am. I may not be there yet, but I can feel her rising. Give me the strength to keep growing, the wisdom to stay aligned with You, and the faith to keep becoming the woman You designed me to be. I am Yours. I am becoming. In Jesus' Name, Amen.

Journal Notes:

Journal Notes:

Day 15:

The Weight You Were Never Meant to Carry

Scripture:

"Come to Me, all who are weary and burdened, and I will give you rest. Take my yoke upon you and learn from me, for I am gentile and humble in heart, and you will find rest for your souls."—Matthew 11:28-29 (NIV)

Devotional Reflection:

There is a kind of tired that sleep can't fix.

It's the kind of exhaustion that seeps into your bones, not just physical fatigue, but soul-weariness. The kind you don't talk about often. The kind that builds up quietly under the surface while you're showing up for everyone else, smiling, managing, leading, parenting, and loving.

But deep down, you're carrying more than anyone knows.

And it's heavy.

You've been the strong one.
The responsible one.

The peacemaker.
The one everyone turns to.

But who do *you* turn to when you're empty? When the weight of holding everything together has started pulling you apart? When the internal pressure to be everything, to be okay all the time, is crushing your spirit?

This isn't just burnout. It's bondage. And you weren't created to live this way.

Jesus' invitation in Matthew 11 isn't just for those who are busy, it's for those who are burdened. It's for the woman who's silently breaking under invisible pressure. He's not calling you to push harder; He's calling you to come closer.

He says, *"Come to Me."*
Not your checklist.
Not your coping mechanism.
Not your performance.
Just *Me.*

God never asked you to carry it all. Somewhere, you picked up weights that were never yours to begin with unrealistic expectations, generational burdens, fear of failure, wounds from the past. You've carried roles, responsibilities, and relationships like armor. And now it's too much.

But beloved, this isn't strength, it's survival. And Jesus is calling you to trade your survival for surrender.

There is rest available, not just for your body, but for your soul. Not temporary relief, but *lasting restoration.*

Imagine this: You, free from the pressure to prove yourself. You, light enough to breathe again. You, surrendered enough to say, "God, I can't carry this anymore. Please take it."

That is holy. That is healing. That is what it means to live in the grace of God, not just the grind of life.

You are not weak because you need rest. You are *wise* when you receive it.

You don't have to earn your way into peace. He already paid for it.

All He asks is that you come with open hands, honest tears, and a heart willing to let go.

Journey Prompts:

1. What invisible weight have you been carrying in silence that you've been afraid to release?

   ____
   ____
   ____
   ____
   ____
   ____

2. Who do you feel responsible for in a way that may be crossing the line from love into burden?

   ____
   ____
   ____
   ____

3. What does true rest look and feel like to your spirit? How can you begin to make space for it?

Prayer:

God, I admit that I am tired, tired of carrying what was never mine to hold. I've worn strength like a mask and independence like a badge of honor, but inside, I am weary. Teach me how to rest in You. Help me lay down the pressure, the perfectionism, the pride, and the pain. I give You everything I've been holding onto so tightly. In return, I receive Your peace. Teach me to walk light, to live open, and to move at the pace of grace. In Jesus' name, amen.

Journal Notes:

Journal Notes:

Day 16:

When Shame Has a Voice

(Story of the Woman Caught in Adultery)

Scripture:

"Then neither do I condemn you," Jesus declared. "Go now and leave your life of sin."—John 8:11 (NIV)

Devotional Reflection:

Shame doesn't knock when it enters, it barges in, loud and accusing. It disguises itself as humility, but it carries the chains of condemnation. Shame whispers in the quiet corners of your mind: *"You should have known better." "You're not worthy." "God can forgive others, but not this."*

It attaches itself to your mistakes, magnifies your missteps, and tries to define your entire identity by a single moment.

That's what they tried to do to *her*, the woman caught in adultery (John 8:1-11). Dragged into the public eye, surrounded by self-righteous judges who held stones in their hands and fury in their hearts. She was vulnerable, exposed, reduced to her worst decision. They didn't care about her repentance; they wanted her ruined.

But Jesus did something radical.

He stooped low to her level, to her shame, to her pain, and began writing in the dirt. We don't know what He wrote, but we know what happened next: one by one, the accusers dropped their stones and walked away.

Then Jesus turned to her with eyes full of compassion and said, *"Where are your accusers? Has no one condemned you?"*

She said, *"No one, sir."*

And He answered, *"Neither do I. Go and sin no more."*

Jesus acknowledged the sin without making her wear it like a name tag. He saw the woman beneath the mistake. He didn't dismiss the call to holiness; He elevated her humanity. He gave her a clean slate and a calling.

Maybe you've been living under shame's shadow. Maybe you've felt like you need to perform self-punishment just to feel worthy again. But Jesus isn't holding a stone, He's holding out His hand.

He knows your full story and still chooses you.

Your past may have shaped you, but it does not have the power to define you. Grace does. And grace always speaks louder than shame.

Journey Prompts:

1. What memories or mistakes still carry the weight of shame in your life?

    ____

    ____

2. How has shame affected the way you see yourself and your relationship with God?

3. What would it look like to fully receive God's forgiveness and release yourself?

Prayer:

Jesus, shame has tried to silence me, label me, and bury me. But You remind me that grace is louder. I lay down my guilt and my self-condemnation at Your feet. Speak truth over my heart and help me walk free. I receive Your forgiveness and declare I am no longer who I was. I am becoming who You've always known I could be. In Jesus' Name, Amen.

Journal Notes:

Day 17:

The Season of Hiddenness

Scripture:

"He made my mouth like a sharpened sword, in the shadow of His hand He hid me; He made me into a polished arrow and concealed me in His quiver."—Isaiah 49:2 (NIV)

Devotional Reflection:

You're doing the work. Praying. Growing. Stretching. Becoming. And yet, it still feels like no one sees you.

There is no spotlight. No stage. No applause. Just quiet. Just obscurity. Just hiddenness.

It can feel like delay. Like punishment. Like rejection. But what if this hidden season is actually *protection*? What if it's *preparation*?

Isaiah 49:2 paints a powerful picture. God makes His servant into a sharpened sword, but then He *hides* it. He polishes an arrow, but keeps it concealed.

Why? Because when you are still being formed, still being sharpened, still being prepared for impact, the worst thing that could happen is premature exposure.

Hiddenness is not a lack of purpose. It is a sacred pause where God deepens your roots and purifies your motives. It is in the dark where seeds grow strong enough to push through the soil. It is in the womb of obscurity where destiny is developed.

You may feel unseen, but you are *not* forgotten. You may feel stuck, but you are *not* behind. You may feel invisible, but you are *being made invincible* in the secret place.

Don't rush the process. Let God complete the hidden work.

Because when it's your time to be revealed, you won't need to strive, you'll be *sent.*

Journey Prompts:

1. What emotions come up when you feel unseen or overlooked?

   ____
   ____
   ____
   ____
   ____
   ____

2. How can you shift your perspective of this season from delay to development?

   ____
   ____
   ____
   ____
   ____
   ____

3. What practices can help you stay spiritually anchored during hiddenness?

____

____

____

____

____

____

Prayer:

God, I confess I've struggled to find purpose in the silence. But now I understand, You are working even when no one sees. Sharpen me. Polish me. Hide me until the appointed time. I trust that what You are doing in the dark will shine in the light. In Jesus' Name, Amen.

Journal Notes:

____

____

____

____

____

____

____

____

____

____

____

____

Journal Notes:

Day 18:

From Bitter to Better

(Story of Naomi)

Scripture:

"Don't call me Naomi," she told them. "Call me Mara, because the Almighty has made my life very bitter."
—Ruth 1:20 (NIV)

Devotional Reflection:

Life can break your heart in ways that make you forget who you are. Naomi knew this all too well. She left Bethlehem full, with a husband, sons, and hope. She returned empty, bitter, and renamed.

"Call me Mara," she said. Bitterness had become her identity.

Loss has a way of reshaping us. Whether it's the death of a loved one, the end of a dream, or the betrayal of someone close, grief can make the past feel like the only place where joy was possible.

But bitterness is a trap. It builds walls around your soul and shuts out the possibility of healing. It convinces you that the pain is safer than the promise.

Yet even in Naomi's brokenness, God was still working.

Through her loyalty to Ruth and Ruth's divine connection to Boaz, Naomi's story began to shift. She became a part of something redemptive. Her legacy was restored. Her hands, once empty, held a baby who would be the ancestor of King David.

God did not erase her pain; He wove purpose through it.

You might not see it now, but the places where you feel most bitter may become the spaces where God reveals His sweetest miracles. Healing is slow. Hope takes courage. But one step toward God in your bitterness can lead to blessings you never imagined.

Your story isn't over. Better is still possible.

Journey Prompts:

1. What area of your life has left a bitter taste in your soul?

   ____
   ____
   ____
   ____
   ____
   ____

2. How have you allowed pain to rename or redefine you?

   ____
   ____
   ____
   ____
   ____

3. What is one small act of hope you can take today toward healing?

Prayer:

Lord, I give You, my bitterness. You see where I've stopped believing in good things. You know the moments that stole my joy. But I choose to return to You, even if I have to come limping. Turn my mourning into meaning. Make my bitter places better. Restore my hope, one moment at a time. In Jesus' Name, Amen.

Journal Notes:

Journal Notes:

Day 19:

Becoming Whole Again

Scripture:

"May God Himself, the God of peace, sanctify you through and through. May your whole spirit, soul and body be kept blameless..."—1 Thessalonians 5:23 (NIV)

Devotional Reflection:

Wholeness isn't about having a perfect life, it's about no longer living a fragmented one.

You were created as a whole being: spirit, soul, and body. But life has a way of breaking that unity. Trauma disconnects you. Shame silences parts of you. Fear freezes your faith. Slowly, your identity fractures, you become the woman who performs but doesn't feel, who serves but doesn't rest, who looks whole but lives hollow.

God is calling you back to *integration.*

He wants to heal your whole self. Not just the church-going, smile-in-public, faith-speaking version of you. But the anxious you. The doubtful you. The tired, wounded, grieving, questioning you.

You don't have to compartmentalize your faith. You can bring every version of yourself to Him.

Healing takes time. It takes grace. It takes God.

When Jesus healed the woman with the issue of blood, He didn't just stop the bleeding. He affirmed her identity: *"Daughter, your faith has made you whole."* (Luke 8:48)

Wholeness isn't a finish line; it's a rhythm of coming back to yourself, back to God, and back to truth every day.

God doesn't want just pieces of you. He wants all of you, unified, undivided, and fully alive.

Journey Prompts:

1. What part of you have you disconnected or suppressed to survive?

   ____
   ____
   ____
   ____
   ____
   ____

2. In what ways do you feel spiritually, emotionally, or physically out of alignment?

   ____
   ____
   ____
   ____
   ____

3. What would it look like to start treating your whole self with kindness and grace?

Prayer:

God of peace, I surrender every fractured part of me into Your hands. Make me whole again. Heal what I hide. Mend what I avoid. Help me live from a place of unity, not brokenness. I receive Your peace to fill every part of who I am. Spirit. Soul. Body. In Jesus' Name, Amen.

Journal Notes:

Journal Notes:

Day 20:

The Gift of Beginning Again

(Story of Rahab)

Scripture:

"By faith the prostitute Rahab, because she welcomed the spies, was not killed..."—Hebrews 11:31 (NIV)

Devotional Reflection:

Rahab wasn't who you'd expect to make it into the Faith Hall of Fame. A prostitute. A Canaanite. An outsider. And yet, *God used her.*

She had a past, but she also had *faith.*

Rahab made a decision to protect the spies from Israel. She risked everything. Her belief in a God she hadn't seen was greater than her fear of the city she knew.

And that one act of courage changed her story.

She wasn't just saved; she became part of the lineage of Jesus Christ.

Rahab reminds us that you are never too far gone to begin again.

You are not your past. You are not your mistakes. You are not what others called you.

You are who *God says you are.*

Every day, you have the opportunity to begin again. To write a new chapter. To choose faith over fear. To step into a future that looks nothing like your past.

Don't disqualify yourself from what God has already marked as yours.

Your new beginning may not be clean. It may come with questions, uncertainty, and trembling steps. But even trembling faith moves mountains.

God is not looking for perfect people, He's looking for willing hearts.

And He'll write a legacy through yours.

Journey Prompts:

1. Where in your life are you afraid to start over?

   ____

   ____

   ____

   ____

   ____

   ____

2. What lies have you believed that have kept you stuck in your past?

____
____
____
____
____
____

3. What truth can you declare today about the woman you are becoming?

____
____
____
____
____
____

Prayer:

God, thank You that with You, it's never too late to begin again. I release every label, every lie, and every limitation that has tried to define me. I choose faith like Rahab. Let my story be one of redemption and courage. Write something beautiful through my yes. In Jesus' Name, Amen.

Journal Notes:

Day 21:

Surrendering the Mask

Scripture:

"You have searched me, Lord, and you know me...before a word is on my tongue you, Lord, know it completely."
—Psalm 139:1,4 (NIV)

Devotional Reflection:

For years, you may have mastered the art of showing up as who others expected you to be. The strong one. The peacemaker. The fixer. The achiever. Somewhere along the way, the version of you that once was authentic slowly became a performance. And while it may have protected you, it also distanced you from your true self.

But pretending is exhausting. Keeping the mask on is a full-time job, and your soul longs for rest. This solo journey isn't about becoming someone new; it's about removing what was never truly you to begin with. Healing begins when you stop performing and start presenting your whole self to God without fear of rejection.

Psalm 139 reminds us that God knows the real you, the raw, unfiltered, no-makeup-on-your-heart version. He knows your words before you speak, your fears before you name them, your pain before you confess it. There is nothing about you that surprises Him. In fact, He delights in your honesty. He isn't looking for the polished version of you, He's pursuing the pure version.

To surrender the mask is to walk in freedom. It is to trust that the real you, the one who's still healing, still hoping, still learning, is worthy of love, belonging, and purpose.

And still, He chooses you.

Let this be the season you surrender the mask. No more hiding behind polished perfection or silent suffering. The woman God called is the one He created, not the one culture tried to curate.

Come into His presence unmasked. Let Him reintroduce you to the woman He sees, beloved, chosen, enough.

Journey Prompts:

1. In what ways have you hidden behind a version of yourself that doesn't feel true anymore?

   ____

   ____

   ____

   ____

   ____

   ____

2. What are the fears that make it hard to let the mask go?

   ____

   ____

   ____

3. What would it feel like to be seen and loved as your full, authentic self?

Prayer:

God, You know me, every layer, every mask, every moment of hiding. I've grown so used to performing that I've forgotten how to just *be*. Today, I lay the mask down. Help me to live in the freedom of authenticity. I want to be the woman You created, not the version I've performed to be accepted. Show me that I am still worthy, even unpolished. Let truth replace fear and wholeness replace pretending. In Jesus' name, Amen.

Journal Notes:

Journal Notes:

Day 22:

Healing the Inner Girl

(Story of the Bleeding Woman)

Scripture:

"Daughter, your faith has healed you. Go in peace and be freed from your suffering."—Mark 5:34 (NIV)

Devotional Reflection:

There's a little girl inside every woman who still longs to be seen, heard, protected, and loved. But too often she was neglected, silenced, or taught to settle. Somewhere along the line, the world told her that vulnerability was weakness and that expressing her needs was too much.

And so, she learned to survive without asking for help. She learned to laugh while hurting, to succeed while silently bleeding, to carry the weight of others while hiding the emptiness in her own heart.

As adults, we often dismiss her pain with statements like, "That was a long time ago," or "I should be over this by now." But Jesus isn't in a hurry. He doesn't dismiss the wounds of the past just because time has passed. He pauses, yes, even in a crowd to heal the deep places that others overlooked. He doesn't rush your story or tell you to move on before you're ready. He meets you in the exact place of your wounding and starts there.

The bleeding woman had been suffering for twelve years. Her condition wasn't just physical, it was emotional, social, and spiritual. She was isolated, labeled "unclean," and likely stripped of her dignity. But she dared to reach for Jesus anyway. She risked public shame for a chance at private healing.

And when she touched Him, He could have let her slip away quietly healed. But Jesus wouldn't let her leave without knowing she was more than her pain. He stopped everything, looked her in the eye, and called her "Daughter."

That word changes everything. Daughter means you belong. It means you are claimed. It means you are loved. It means you have a place, not because of what you've done, but because of who you are to Him.

Jesus isn't just healing symptoms; He's healing the story. He goes to the root. He addresses the abandonment, the betrayal, the unmet needs, the silenced cries, and the stolen innocence. He speaks life to the parts of you that you thought were too shattered to be whole again.

And when He heals, He restores. He gives back what was taken, peace where there was torment, dignity where there was shame, joy where there was mourning.

Today, He wants to meet the inner girl in you who was overlooked, rejected, or made to feel small. He wants to hold her face in His hands and remind her, "You are Mine." He wants to speak truth over her lies, safety over her fears, and worth over her wounds.

Healing may be messy. It may bring tears before it brings relief. But you are not doing it alone. The same Jesus who stopped for the bleeding woman will stop for you every single time.

Journey Prompts:

1. What memory from your younger self still feels unresolved or painful?

____
____
____
____
____
____

2. What would that little girl inside you say she needed back then?

____
____
____
____
____
____

3. What do you want Jesus to say to her now?

____
____
____
____
____
____

Prayer:

Jesus, thank You for caring about the little girl in me, the one who was hurt, unseen, silenced, or afraid. Today, I bring her to You. I give You every wound I've buried and every tear I never cried. Speak to the deepest parts of me. Reparent the places I've hidden. Let Your love reach all the way back to the moments that shaped me and let healing begin from the inside out. In Jesus' Name, Amen.

Journal Notes:

Journal Notes:

Day 23: Breaking the Cycle

Scripture:

"To be made new in the attitude of your minds; and to put on the new self, created to be like God in true righteousness and holiness."—Ephesians 4:23-24 (NIV)

Devotional Reflection:

Sometimes, freedom doesn't look like a sudden breakthrough, it looks like daily choices to do things differently. It looks like saying "no" to what's familiar and "yes" to what is healthy, even when it's uncomfortable.

We all inherit patterns. Maybe yours include silence instead of expression, survival instead of intimacy, or control instead of trust. Sometimes the dysfunction we grew up in became so familiar, it started to feel normal. But generational patterns can end with you. You may have inherited the pain, but you get to choose the future.

Breaking the cycle might feel lonely at first. It may require boundaries. It may stir resistance from those who benefited from your silence. But it will also bring freedom. And not just for you, but for those coming after you.

God is doing a *new thing* in you. That means your story isn't over. In fact, this is the beginning of something sacred. A turning point. A holy interruption.

To fully embrace the new, you must stop rehearsing the old. That means releasing shame, letting go of familiar pain, and stepping into healing, even when it's uncomfortable.

You are called to be the turning point in your story, to trade trauma for truth, reaction for reflection, and pain for purpose. Keep choosing differently. Keep showing up. Your breakthrough is in your consistency.

Journey Prompts:

1. What generational or personal patterns are you determined to end?

   ____
   ____
   ____
   ____
   ____
   ____

2. What new habits, mindsets, or boundaries is God calling you to create?

   ____
   ____
   ____
   ____
   ____
   ____

3. What truth can you cling to when the old cycle tries to call you back?

   ____
   ____

Prayer:

God, I declare that the cycle ends with me. I may not have chosen the pain I inherited, but I choose what I pass down. Strengthen me to walk in newness, even when it's unfamiliar. Break every lie that tells me I'm stuck or unworthy of change. Empower me to be the bridge between what was and what will be. I thank You that I'm not doing this alone. I am covered by grace and led by truth. In Jesus' name, Amen.

Journal Notes:

Journal Notes:

Day 24:

Embracing Sacred Solitude

(Story of Mary Magdalene)

Scripture:

"Now Mary stood outside the tomb crying... Jesus said to her, 'Mary.' She turned toward Him... "—John 20:11,16 (NIV)

Devotional Reflection:

There is a difference between being alone and being *with* God in solitude. Sacred solitude is not isolation, it is invitation. In solitude, we don't just listen for God, we encounter Him.

Mary Magdalene knew the power of that space. After everything, His death, the silence, the loss of purpose, she stood at the tomb, weeping. She stayed. She didn't run. She wasn't distracted by the noise or overwhelmed by the unknown. She simply stayed in the ache.

And it was there, in the quiet ache of solitude, that Jesus met her. He didn't meet her in a crowd. He didn't need her to prove anything. He simply spoke her name.

Your greatest revelations often come not when you're surrounded by people, but when you're still enough to hear your name called in the quiet.

Solitude is where your spirit is recalibrated. It's where clarity returns. It's where the noise of the world fades and the voice of God becomes unmistakably clear. Today's society glorifies connection, solitude becomes a radical act of healing.

You don't have to fear the quiet. Because in the quiet, you're never alone, you're deeply met.

Journey Prompts:

1. How do you typically respond to being alone, do you resist it or welcome it? Why?

   ____
   ____
   ____
   ____
   ____
   ____

2. What is God revealing to you in this current season of solitude?

   ____
   ____
   ____
   ____
   ____
   ____

3. What can you release in this quiet space that you've been clinging to in the noise?

   ____
   ____
   ____
   ____

Prayer:

Lord, teach me to embrace solitude as sacred. Help me quiet the noise around me so I can hear Your still, small voice. In the places where I've feared being alone, show me that I am fully met by You. Let this quiet place become holy ground where transformation begins. Speak my name like You did to Mary. Let me know You and myself more deeply in the stillness. In Jesus' name, Amen.

Journal Notes:

Journal Notes:

Day 25:

Reclaiming Your Voice

Scripture:

"She speaks with wisdom, and faithful instruction is on her tongue."—Proverbs 31:26 (NIV)

Devotional Reflection:

Somewhere along the way, life taught you to stay silent. Maybe your ideas were dismissed. Maybe you were told, "You're too emotional," or, "You're being dramatic." Maybe you were shamed for speaking up or made to feel like your presence was too much.

So, you began shrinking. Editing yourself. Swallowing your truth to keep the peace. Smiling when you wanted to cry. Dimmed light felt safer than shining.

But silence has a cost. Over time, you start to forget the sound of your own voice. You begin to believe that your story doesn't matter, that your perspective isn't valuable, that your truth isn't worth the space it takes up. That is a lie from the enemy.

From the very beginning, God's creative power was released through words: "Let there be light." And there was light. Words shape worlds and the enemy knows it. That's why he works so hard to convince you to keep quiet. Because your voice is dangerous to darkness.

God gave you a voice, not just to be heard, but to bring life. To speak truth in love. To declare His promises over your family, your future, and yourself. To tear down lies and build up faith.

In Proverbs 31, the woman's voice is described as carrying both wisdom and kindness. Notice it's not just truth, it's truth wrapped in grace. That's what makes it powerful. That's what makes it healing.

Look at Esther. She could have stayed silent. She could have kept her position and her safety. But when Mordecai reminded her, "Who knows but that you have come to your royal position for such a time as this?"—she found the courage to speak. And her words saved a nation.

Your voice was never meant to be hidden. It was meant to shift atmospheres. To disrupt injustice. To empower the next generation. To advocate for the voiceless. To tell your story so someone else knows they're not alone.

Speak, daughter. Not to impress. Not to dominate. But to heal. Let your voice be an echo of heaven, firm, yet gentle; bold, yet humble.

Because here's the truth:
Your silence won't protect you. But your voice? It might set someone else free. And in the process, it just might set you free too.

Journal Prompts:

1. When did you first begin to feel like your voice didn't matter?

   ____

   ____

2. What truth do you need to remind yourself of every time fear tempts you to stay silent?

3. Where in your life is God asking you to speak up, show up, or share your truth?

Prayer:

God, thank You for the voice You placed inside me. Forgive me for the times I silenced myself out of fear or doubt. Today, I reclaim my voice, not in arrogance, but in confidence. Let my words carry grace, wisdom, and healing. Let me speak not to impress but to uplift. I am no longer shrinking, I am rising. Let every word I speak reflect Your light. In Jesus' name, Amen.

Journal Notes:

Day 26:

Letting Go of Control

Scripture:

" Therefore I tell you, do not worry about your life, what you will eat or drink, or about your body, what you will wear. Is not life more than food and the body more than clothes? Look at the birds in the air; they do not sow, or reap, or store away in barns, and yet your heavenly Father feeds them. Are you not much more valuable than they?"
—Matthew 6:25-26 (NIV)

Devotional Reflection:

Control can feel like protection. It gives the illusion of safety, order, and predictability. When life feels uncertain, we reach for the steering wheel, desperate to feel like we're doing something to hold it all together. But when we grip too tightly, we often crowd out the gentle nudges of God. The more you cling to your plans, the less room you leave for His miracles.

And let's be honest, control feels powerful… until it doesn't. It works until the job changes, the diagnosis comes, the relationship ends, or the unexpected bill arrives. Then, the very thing you thought would keep you safe leaves you exhausted and anxious.

Underneath that need for control is often a deeper root: fear. Fear of being abandoned, disappointed, or caught off guard.

Fear that if you don't manage it all, everything will fall apart. But here's the truth, sister: control doesn't protect you; it imprisons you. It traps you in cycles of overthinking and wears you down with the weight of what you were never meant to carry.

Letting go of control is not about giving up, it's about trusting up. It's loosening your grip on the pen and allowing God to write the story. It's saying, "God, I don't understand this, but I believe You're still good."

Look at the birds. They aren't planning next month's meals or calculating their savings. They just wake up and live in the provision of their Creator. And yet, God calls you more valuable than they. If He cares for sparrows, He will certainly care for you.

Surrender is the soil where miracles grow. When you let go, you stop trying to force outcomes and start making space for divine intervention. You begin to see how God's plans far surpass your own. You walk in peace that makes no logical sense but feels like home.

The cross itself is the ultimate picture of surrender. Jesus didn't fight to control the outcome; He trusted His Father with it. And from that surrender came the greatest victory in history.

He will never lead you where His grace won't keep you. You are safe in His hands, even when the path is unclear. So, breathe deep. Release your grip. Rest in the truth that surrender is not weakness, it is the birthplace of strength, freedom, and miracles.

Journal Prompts:

1. What areas of your life have you been trying to control?

   ____

   ____

   ____

   ____

   ____

   ____

2. What would it look like to release those into God's hands?

   ____

   ____

   ____

   ____

   ____

   ____

3. How would your life feel if you truly believed God was in control?

   ____

   ____

   ____

   ____

   ____

   ____

Prayer:

God, I confess that I've been holding on too tightly. I release the pressure to have all the answers and to make everything work on my own. I trust You to guide me, even when the path isn't clear. Help me walk in surrendered peace. In Jesus' name, Amen.

Journal Notes:

Journal Notes:

Day 27:

Becoming Whole

(Story of the Samaritan Woman)

Scripture:

"Then, leaving her water jar, the woman went back to the town and said to the people, 'Come, see a man who told me everything I ever did.'"—John 4:28–29 (NIV)

Devotional Reflection:

The Samaritan woman was tired, tired of hiding, tired of avoiding, tired of carrying shame she didn't know how to shake. She came to the well for water, but she left with something far greater; healing, wholeness, and the freedom to be seen and still loved.

Day after day, she walked to the well in the heat of the day alone, avoiding the whispers, dodging the judgment, covering the scars that life had left behind. Her past was a weight she had grown used to carrying, but not without cost. Her heart was weary. Her spirit was worn. And still… Jesus met her there.

He didn't flinch at her story. He didn't shame her or define her by her past. He looked her in the eyes, saw her soul, and spoke to her with dignity. That moment shifted everything. Her identity wasn't "rejected," "divorced," or "unworthy" anymore. She became "known," "chosen," and "sent."

Jesus didn't just tell her the truth about her life; He revealed the truth about her identity. And with that revelation, she did something symbolic: she left behind her water jar. The very vessel she used to survive… she abandoned it. Because what she received from Jesus was far more life-giving than anything she could draw from a well.

What's in your jar? What are you still carrying to cope, to earn love, to stay afloat, shame, fear, perfectionism, comparison, addiction, silence, busyness? What's keeping you from walking fully in freedom?

Becoming whole means releasing the broken labels and allowing God to rewrite your story. It means surrendering the identity that pain assigned you and reclaiming the one God originally intended. It's choosing to believe that your past doesn't disqualify you, it equips you. That your scars don't make you too damaged, they make you deeply usable.

The moment you stop hiding is the moment you start healing. And healing doesn't mean forgetting what happened, it means refusing to let it define you any longer.

You don't have to have it all together to be used by God. He's calling you forward, even now with full knowledge of your past. Because your brokenness is not a barrier. It's the beginning of breakthrough. And like the Samaritan woman, you have a testimony that can set others free.

You are not who you were. You are not what they said. You are who He calls you: daughter, redeemed, and whole.

Journal Prompts:

1. What labels or lies have you believed about yourself that God is now replacing?

   ____

   ____

2. What "water jar" are you being invited to leave behind today?

3. What does wholeness look like to you?

Prayer:

Jesus, thank You for seeing me beyond my past. I've carried shame for too long. I'm ready to drop the jar and pick up my purpose. Heal the parts of me I've hidden. Restore the pieces that feel broken. And help me walk forward as the woman You call whole. In Your name, Amen.

Journal Notes:

Day 28:

Redefining Success

Scripture:

"Do not conform to the pattern of this world, but be transformed by the renewing of your mind."

—Romans 12:2 (NIV)

Devotional Reflection:

The world defines success as fame, fortune, recognition, and productivity. It's measured by the size of your following, the weight of your bank account, the title on your business card, or how many people applaud when you walk into the room. But God defines success by an entirely different standard; obedience, faithfulness, surrender, and intimacy with Him.

Success in the Kingdom isn't loud, it's lasting. It's not flashy, it's faithful. It doesn't scream for attention; it quietly transforms hearts.

God is far more interested in your character than your clout. In your spiritual fruit than your social following. In your willingness to say "yes" when no one's watching than in how many people see your highlight reel. Because in Heaven's economy, private obedience carries more weight than public approval.

Success is not in being busy, it's in being aligned. It's not in comparison, it's in completion. When you chase what the world celebrates, you will always come up empty. But when you chase what God commands, you find fulfillment, peace, and purpose.

On your solo journey, God is inviting you to shift your perspective. The pressure to perform, to prove, to keep up, it was never yours to carry. You are not what you produce. You are not your performance. You are not your accomplishments. You are a beloved daughter of the King.

Your worth is not based on your status, your income, or your to-do list. It is anchored in your identity. Heaven doesn't measure success by outcomes; it measures it by obedience. Were you faithful when it was hard? Did you love when it was inconvenient? Did you trust when it didn't make sense?

You may never get a trophy for the late-night prayer, the quiet forgiveness, or the obedience no one sees, but those are the moments that make you powerful in the Kingdom. Those are the unseen seeds that produce eternal fruit.

Success is showing up even when it's unseen. It's giving your best even when there's no applause. It's being faithful to the assignment God gave you, whether it makes sense or not.

Keep showing up. Keep being faithful. Keep saying "yes" to God. That is success.

Journal Prompts:

1. Whose definition of success have you been living by?

   ____

   ____

   ____

   ____

   ____

2. What is one area where you can choose faithfulness over performance?

3. What would success look like if you measured it by peace, not productivity?

Prayer:

Lord, I've spent too much time chasing what the world told me matters. Help me see success the way You do. Teach me to value purpose over praise and obedience over outcomes. I choose to let go of comparison and trust that faithfulness is enough. In Jesus' name, Amen.

Journal Notes:

Day 29:

Freedom to Feel

Scripture:

"The Lord is close to the brokenhearted and saves those who are crushed in spirit."—Psalm 34:18 (NIV)

Devotional Reflection:

Somewhere, you were taught that crying makes you weak. That emotions are a liability. That if you just "stay strong," you'll survive. But survival is not the goal; healing is. You were not created to endure life in silence or to carry your pain beneath layers of forced smiles and unspoken grief. You were created to live freely, and part of freedom is feeling.

Somewhere along the way, many women were told to be "good girls", quiet, agreeable, pleasant. Not too loud. Not too emotional. So, we silenced our pain to be palatable. We shut down our anger to be accepted. We buried our sadness to stay functional. And in doing so, we disconnected from a part of ourselves that God fully intended to be part of our spiritual experience: our emotions.

God never asked you to bury your feelings. He asked you to bring them to Him. He's the safest place for your sorrow, your anger, your disappointment, your confusion. He doesn't shame your tears; He bottles them (Psalm 56:8 NLT). He doesn't run from your brokenness; He draws closer.

Your emotions are not interruptions to your spiritual life. They are invitations. Invitations to be comforted, to be understood, to be healed. They are signals from your soul, whispering, "Something here still needs your attention. Something here still needs God's touch."

You were created to feel deeply, not to be controlled by your emotions, but to honor them. To sit with them, invite Jesus into them, and allow His love to minister to the raw and vulnerable parts of you. Because in acknowledging what you feel, you give space for what God wants to do. You can't heal what you don't admit hurts. You can't overcome what you keep pretending doesn't exist.

Let today be the day you give yourself permission to feel again. To cry without apology. To grieve without guilt. To rest without proving. To breathe without fear. Your tears are not a sign of weakness; they are a sign of release. A holy unraveling that makes room for God's comfort and restoration.

He is not afraid of your emotional waves; He walks on them. He does not despise your breakdowns; He meets you in them. Your feelings matter. And God is close, even in the tear-soaked moments. Especially in the tear-soaked moments.

Journal Prompts:

1. What emotions have you been avoiding, and why?

   ____

   ____

   ____

   ____

   ____

   ____

2. How has suppressing your feelings affected your spiritual or emotional health?

____

____

____

____

____

____

3. What would emotional honesty with God look like for you?

____

____

____

____

____

____

Prayer:

God, I bring You every feeling I've tried to hide. You see the tears I've never cried and the pain I've never named. Help me to feel without shame and to trust that You're with me in every emotion. Thank You for being close. Thank You for holding me when I can't hold myself. In Jesus' name, Amen.

Journal Notes:

____

____

____

Journal Notes:

Day 30:

Becoming Her

Scripture:

"The Lord will fulfill his purpose for me; your steadfast love, O Lord, endures forever. Do not forsake the work of your hands."— Psalm 138:8 (ESV)

Devotional Reflection:

You are becoming her, the woman God dreamed about when He formed you. The one who walks in confidence, speaks with wisdom, prays with authority, and loves from a healed place. The one who knows who she is, not because life has been easy, but because God has been faithful.

Becoming her is not a destination, it's a daily decision. It's choosing to rise each morning with intention, even when you're tired. It's choosing healing over hardness, softness over shame, and purpose over people-pleasing. It's choosing to speak life when you used to speak fear. To take up space when you once shrunk to fit into someone else's comfort zone.

This journey is not about becoming impressive, it's about becoming intimate with your Creator. It's not about reaching a place of perfection, it's about walking in increasing wholeness. Becoming her means you trust God in the middle, not just at the mountaintop. You trust His timing, His process, and His hand, even when it feels slow, unclear, or painful.

God is doing a good work in you. Not a rushed work. Not a shallow work. But a deep, lasting, transforming work. He is pruning the lies, healing the wounds, restoring the dreams, and rewriting the parts of your story you once wanted to erase. Some days you may not see the progress. You might feel stuck, uncertain, or even unworthy. But Heaven sees it. Heaven records every tear, every act of surrender, every secret "yes."

And make no mistake: your *becoming* is not fragile, it's holy.

You don't have to wait until you're "finished" to walk in purpose. You don't have to have it all figured out to make an impact. You are becoming her *right now*; messy, holy, stretched, strengthened, refined, and renewed. Every "yes" you whisper, every fear you face, every lie you silence, every truth you reclaim brings you one step closer.

Becoming her means embracing your process and letting God shape you from the inside out. It's knowing that what He began in you, He's faithful to finish. Even when it's slow. Even when it's quiet. Even when no one else sees it.

Keep going. Don't stop. Don't despise your process. Don't discount your progress. You are not behind, you are becoming. And the woman you're stepping into has been waiting for you to believe she was already inside you all along.

God finishes what He starts, and beloved, He started something beautiful in you.

Journal Prompts:

1. Describe the woman you are becoming. What qualities is God awakening in you?

   ____

   ____

2. What progress have you made that you may have overlooked?

3. What would it look like to fully embrace the process, even when it's uncomfortable?

Prayer:

God, thank You that I don't have to have it all together to be loved or used by You. I am becoming the woman You created me to be. Strengthen me for the journey, remind me that You're not finished, and help me to trust the process even on the hard days. I give You full permission to shape me into her. In Jesus' name, Amen.

Journal Notes:

Day 31:
Rediscovering Wonder

Scripture:

"Unless you change and become like little children, you will never enter the kingdom of heaven."—Matthew 18:3 (NIV)

Devotional Reflection:

Somewhere along the road of survival, striving, and responsibility, many women lose their sense of wonder. The fire in your eyes becomes dimmed by deadlines. The creativity once bubbling inside gets replaced with to-do lists. The questions that once stirred your curiosity now echo in the silence of fear and overthinking.

You may have traded dreaming for duty. You learned how to be efficient but forgot how to be enchanted. You became so good at holding it all together, you forgot how to be held.

But Jesus invites you to return, not to childish ways, but to *childlike faith.* To believe again. To hope again. To wonder again.

Rediscovering wonder is not about escaping your responsibilities, it's about awakening your spirit. It means looking at your life not through the lens of what's missing, but through the lens of what's *possible.* It means seeing with your soul, not just your eyes. It means believing that even in the mundane, God is working miracles. He's in the quiet sigh after a long day, in the unexpected encouragement, in the laughter that bubbles up from nowhere.

God wants to restore your sense of awe, not just in who He is, but in who *you* are in Him. You are His daughter. You are a vessel of creativity, light, and divine potential. And that playful, trusting, imaginative part of you, the one who danced before life got complicated, is still in there.

This is your invitation to be present enough to *see* again. To feel again. To laugh until your belly hurts. To ask bold questions. To say "wow" again at the kindness of God in the little things. Because when wonder is restored, faith expands. Fear loosens. Creativity flows. And healing begins.

You don't have to know how it ends to trust the Author. He writes redemption into every chapter. And today, He is inviting you to rediscover the beauty that has always been there waiting for your attention.

Journal Prompts:

1. When was the last time you felt a deep sense of wonder or awe?

   ____

   ____

   ____

   ____

   ____

   ____

2. What parts of your life feel dull or routine that God may be inviting you to view with fresh eyes?

   ____

   ____

3. What would it look like to approach your life with childlike trust this week?

Prayer:

God, awaken my heart to wonder again. Help me slow down enough to notice Your beauty, Your fingerprints, and Your movement in my life. Restore my childlike faith and teach me to trust You even when I don't understand. Let me dream again. In Jesus' name, Amen.

Journal Notes:

Journal Notes:

Day 32:

The Courage to Be Seen

(Story of the Woman with the Alabaster Jar)

Scripture:

"She has done a beautiful thing to me."—Mark 14:6 (NIV)

Devotional Reflection:

The woman with the alabaster jar wasn't invited to the table. She didn't have the right status, reputation, or credentials. But she came anyway boldly, vulnerably, worshipfully. She poured out her most costly offering; tears, oil, dignity, and in doing so, she was seen, honored, and remembered by Jesus.

She didn't come with eloquent words or a carefully planned appearance. She came with her pain, her passion, and her heart wide open. She entered a room that likely whispered about her, judged her, even tried to dismiss her. But her focus wasn't on them, it was on Him.

It takes courage to be seen. To bring your full self; past, pain, worship, weakness into the presence of others and of God. But breakthrough lives on the other side of vulnerability. And true freedom begins when you stop hiding.

We often spend years editing ourselves, toning down our voices, hiding our hurt, rehearsing our worth in the mirror. But

God is not impressed by performance. He is moved by authenticity. By a heart that says, "Here I am, mess and all."

You are not too much. You are not too broken. You are not too far gone. Your worship is beautiful. Your surrender is sacred. Your truth is enough.

God isn't waiting for you to clean yourself up, He's waiting for you to come as you are. And just like that woman, your story will be remembered not for how polished it looked, but for how powerfully you loved and how fully you showed up.

Let her story remind you: your past doesn't disqualify you. In fact, it may be the very thing God uses to pour healing into others. Your scars speak. Your tears speak. Your presence is prophetic.

Being seen is risky. But it's also the place where shame loses its grip, healing takes root, and the oil of your anointing begins to flow.

So come. Unedited. Unfiltered. Undone. Because *this* is what worship looks like.

Journal Prompts:

1. Where in your life have you been hiding or holding back?

   ____

   ____

   ____

   ____

   ____

   ____

2. What would it look like to show up fully, honestly, and boldly today?

____

____

____

____

____

____

3. What part of your story might God want to use to bless someone else?

____

____

____

____

____

____

Prayer:

Jesus, I bring You my whole self, nothing hidden, nothing held back. Give me the courage to be seen and to know that I am fully loved in the process. Let my life be a living testimony of grace, freedom, and worship. In Jesus' Name, Amen.

Journal Notes:

____

____

____

____

Journal Notes:

Day 33:

When the Wilderness Finds You

Scripture:

"Therefore, I am now going to allure her; I will lead her into the wilderness and speak tenderly to her."
—Hosea 2:14 (NIV)

Devotional Reflection:

The wilderness is not punishment, it's preparation. It's the sacred place where God strips away the noise so you can hear His voice again. It's where your false identities fall off and your true self begins to emerge.

It may feel lonely. You may wonder why everything familiar had to fall apart. Why doors closed. Why people left. But sometimes, the wilderness is the very place where God allures you, where He draws you into deeper intimacy. He doesn't shout in the wilderness; He whispers. He speaks tenderly. Because it's not about the destination. It's about what's being developed in you.

The wilderness dismantles idols you didn't know you had, security in titles, validation from others, dependence on your own strength. It exposes what's been numbing you and calls you into a raw, holy dependence on God alone. Here, you discover that your worth isn't attached to doing, achieving, or impressing. You are loved simply because you are His.

In the wilderness, you learn to be. To breathe. To receive. You learn that God's presence is not limited to the mountaintop moments, it meets you right in the desert with daily manna, living water, and whispers of hope.

This is the place where layers fall off, layers of performance, perfectionism, fear, and shame. What emerges is a woman more rooted, more radiant, more real. You begin to understand that being stripped down is not the same as being left behind, it's being *refined.*

Don't despise the wilderness. Don't rush it. Let it do its holy work in you. Let it quiet your soul and reignite your spirit. Let it draw you closer to the God who doesn't waste a single tear, a single pause, a single detour.

He is writing something sacred in the dry places. He is building your strength. He is restoring your voice. He is preparing you for what's next.

So, walk slowly. Listen closely. The wilderness is not the end of your story, it's where the next chapter begins.

Journal Prompts:

1. What has the wilderness season revealed about who you are and what you've depended on? Reflect on the identities, habits, or attachments that have been stripped away during this time.

   ____
   ____
   ____
   ____

____

____

2. Where have you sensed God's whisper in your wilderness? Describe a moment when you felt God's presence in a quiet, unexpected, or deeply personal way.

____

____

____

____

____

____

3. What do you believe God is preparing you for in this season? Consider how He might be strengthening your faith, shifting your perspective, or stretching your capacity.

____

____

____

____

____

____

Prayer:

God, I confess that the wilderness has felt hard, confusing, and at times, lonely. But I trust that You are not punishing me, you are preparing me. Thank You for stripping away what was never meant to define me. Thank You for whispering to me in the quiet, for meeting me with tender mercy instead of judgment. Help me to lean into this season without rushing out of it. Refine me, restore me, and reveal what I could not see in the noise of life. Remind me that this wilderness is not a detour, it's divine. I am listening, Lord. Speak. In Jesus' name, Amen.

Journal Notes:

Journal Notes:

Day 34:

Rebuilding with God

Scripture:

"Unless the Lord builds the house, the builders labor in vain."—Psalm 127:1 (NIV)

Devotional Reflection:

You've torn down walls. You've let go of lies. You've faced your past. And now, it's time to rebuild. But this time, you won't do it alone.

This is not about returning to who you used to be, it's about becoming who you were always meant to be. The woman who rises from the rubble with grace in her stride and glory in her story. The woman who no longer builds from insecurity or fear, but from trust, healing, and purpose.

Rebuilding with God means letting Him be the architect of your identity, the foundation of your confidence, and the source of your wisdom. You're not just putting pieces back together, you're laying new bricks on truth, grace, and purpose. He is not trying to restore your comfort zone; He's creating a new zone of calling, wholeness, and holy impact.

And yes, rebuilding is vulnerable. Sometimes it feels like starting over. But this time, you're not building with shaky materials like people-pleasing, perfectionism, or pain. You are building on the Rock. The Cornerstone. The One who cannot be moved.

This is where restoration begins, not in trying to recreate what was, but in surrendering to what *can be.* Let go of the comparison. The timelines. The fear that it's too late. God redeems time. He repurposes pain. And what He builds through you will not crumble, because He is both the Builder and the Sustainer.

The life God is building through you may not look like anyone else's, but it will be solid, sacred, and strong. He sees the blueprint. He holds the vision. You just have to keep saying yes.

God doesn't rebuild halfway. He rebuilds beautifully, fully, and with eternal vision. So don't be afraid to dream again. To love again. To trust again. To *become* again. Because this time, you're not rebuilding from survival, you're rebuilding from *surrender.*

And with surrender comes strength. With surrender comes strategy. With surrender comes the kind of peace you never thought you'd find again. This is your sacred rebuild. And it starts now.

Journal Prompts:

1. What has God torn down or asked you to release in this season?

   ____

   ____

   ____

   ____

   ____

____

2. What do you sense He is inviting you to rebuild with Him?

____
____
____
____
____
____

3. What does a God-built life look like to you?

____
____
____
____
____
____

Prayer:

Lord, I give You full access to every broken place. Rebuild me, not in my strength but in Yours. Be the foundation of my identity, my dreams, and my relationships. I trust You to create something stronger and more beautiful than what I could ever build on my own. In Jesus' name, Amen.

Journal Notes:

Day 35:

The Gift of Now

Scripture:

"This is the day the Lord has made; let us rejoice and be glad in it."—Psalm 118:24 (NLT)

Devotional Reflection:

On this solo journey, it can be tempting to live in the past, mourning what you lost, replaying old conversations, or rehearsing regrets. Or maybe you find yourself leaning too far forward, consumed with what's next, anxious about tomorrow, planning for outcomes, and wondering if things will ever come together.

But healing happens in the *now*. Peace lives in the *present*. Joy is a gift God offers you *today*.

You don't have to wait until everything is figured out to be present in your life. You don't have to be whole to be joyful. You don't need every detail of your story resolved to receive the beauty of this moment. You can honor this day, this breath, this breakthrough, this small miracle, as sacred. This is the day God is walking with you. This is the day that grace still flows and mercies are made new. This is the day the journey turns inward, toward gratitude.

There is power in presence. There is power in slowing down long enough to feel your heartbeat and realize that you are still here. Still becoming. Still chosen. There is power in laughing without apology, crying without shame, and choosing joy without needing a reason.

This is not just another ordinary day, it's a divine invitation. An invitation to dwell. To taste your coffee with intention. To feel your breath and know God gave it. To hold space for your healing without rushing it. To say thank you for what is *still* good.

The enemy wants to keep you distracted, by regret, by pressure, by timelines that don't honor your pace. But God is not bound by the clocks we chase. He is here. In the room. In the silence. In the stillness.

He's not just the God of your past and your future; He is the God of your *now*. He is writing your story in real time. And even if you don't feel like it's all coming together, it's still unfolding according to His plan.

Let today be enough. Let it be holy. Let it be seen. Don't miss the gift of this moment trying to fix yesterday or predict tomorrow. Breathe it in. Bless it. And embrace the now as the sacred space where healing begins and miracles unfold.

Journal Prompts:

1. Where have you been mentally living in the past or in the future?

   ____

   ____

   ____

   ____

   ____

2. What is something small but beautiful about *today*?

3. How can you practice presence and gratitude more intentionally this week?

Prayer:

God, thank You for this moment. Help me not to miss what You are doing because I'm too focused on what was or what might be. Teach me to live fully in the present, trusting that You are here and that today is enough. In Jesus' name, Amen.

Journal Notes:

Journal Notes:

Day 36:

Anchored in Identity

Scripture:

"For you created my inmost being; you knit me together in my mother's womb. I praise you because I am fearfully and wonderfully made; your works are wonderful, I know that full well. My frame was not hidden from you when I was made in the secret place, when I was woven together in the depths of the earth. Your eyes saw my unformed body; all the days ordained for me were written in your book before one of them came to be. ."—Psalm 139:13-16 (NIV)

Devotional Reflection:

There comes a point in every woman's life when she looks at herself and wonders, "Who am I, really?" Not the titles, not the roles, not the version of herself shaped by survival, but the soul that longs to be known, chosen, and loved just as she is.

Identity is not about what you do, how others see you, or even who you were in the past, it's about who God declares you to be. And He doesn't just assign you a name, He calls you by it. That means He speaks into your becoming. Even when you feel lost, your true self is not forgotten by the One who formed you.

So much of your pain may be rooted in a crisis of identity. Maybe people labeled you difficult, needy, broken. Maybe your self-worth was tied to someone else's love or approval. Maybe the version of you that others accepted was really just a mask. And when that mask no longer served you, you were left wondering, Who am I without it?

God answers that question not by pointing to your past, but by pointing to Himself. "You are Mine." That is identity. That is security. That is love.

He doesn't say you are what you've done or what you've been through. He says you are redeemed. You are not your trauma. You are not your mistakes. You are not who they said you were. You are God's beloved daughter, called by name, not a number, not a label, not a case. You are His. Fully known, fully seen, fully loved.

And here's the thing, when you start walking in that truth, the need for comparison loses its grip. The approval of others stops being your lifeline. You stop chasing worthiness and start living from it. You realize you were never created to fit in; you were created to stand out as a reflection of God's glory.

On this solo journey, God is peeling back the layers that life has placed on you. The shame. The fear. The false identities. He's bringing you face-to-face with the woman He always saw, even when you couldn't see her yourself. And that woman? She's radiant. She's free. She's anchored in the truth that her worth is not up for debate, it was settled at the cross.

So today, let this be your declaration: "I am who God says I am. Nothing less. Nothing more. And that is enough."

Journal Prompts:

1. Where did you first begin to question or lose your identity?

   ____

2. What labels or roles have you taken on that no longer serve the woman God is calling you to be?

3. What would it look like to live from a place of knowing deeply that you belong to God?

Prayer:

Father, I've worn so many names that weren't mine. I've tried to be who others needed, who they preferred, who they praised, but I've forgotten who You say I am. Today, I release every false identity and root myself in the truth that I am Yours. Redeemed. Known. Loved. Called by name. Anchor me in this identity so deeply that nothing can shake it. In Jesus' name, Amen.

Journal Notes:

Day 37:

Courage to Confront

Scripture:

"Search me, God, and know my heart; test me and know my anxious thoughts."—Psalm 139:23 (NIV)

Devotional Reflection:

Sometimes the scariest place to stand is in front of the mirror, not just the glass one, but the mirror of your heart. Because in that still, silent place, there's no hiding. No pretending. No carefully curated version of yourself to present to the world. It's just you, your truth, and God.

But what if that confrontation wasn't punishment?

What if it was an invitation?

There's a version of you that's been buried, layered under years of being the strong one, the dependable one, the peacemaker, the one who absorbs everyone else's pain so no one else has to. You've been applauded for it, but deep down, you know it's been costing you something. The mirror doesn't lie, but it doesn't have to accuse either. It can become a sacred meeting place, a sanctuary where healing begins.

When you dare to look deeply, you may see the little girl still carrying disappointments she never voiced. You may see the woman who has mastered smiling while silently aching. And you may see the soul, still reaching, still longing, still hoping.

David's prayer in Psalm 139 wasn't casual, it was courageous. "Search me, God, and know my heart; test me and know my anxious thoughts." That's not a prayer for the faint of heart. It's saying:

Lord, go past my polished answers. Go past the part of me I've learned to make presentable. Put Your hand on the tender spots I've hidden, the fears I've rationalized, and the shame I've tried to forget. Not to condemn me, but to free me.

Sometimes the most powerful act of faith is not charging ahead in busyness, but standing still in God's light and saying, "Here I am. All of me. Even the parts I'm scared to look at."

And here's the truth, there is no dark corner of your heart that His light cannot reach. There is no wound too deep for His hands to touch. And there is no truth about you that will make Him turn away.

So, look in the mirror, not to criticize, but to recognize. Let it reflect both your humanity and His holiness at work within you. Let it remind you that you are safe to be fully seen and fully loved. The mirror can show you where you are, but God will show you who you are becoming.

And this time, you don't have to hide anymore.

Journal Prompts:

1. What emotions arise when you truly look at yourself without filters; physically, emotionally, spiritually?

____
____
____
____
____
____

2. What parts of your heart have you been afraid for God (or others) to see?

____
____
____
____
____
____

3. If Jesus stood beside you in the mirror, what might He say to you right now?

____
____
____
____
____
____

Prayer:

Lord, give me the courage to be honest with myself. Not so I can tear myself down, but so I can finally build from truth. Search me. Know me. Show me the parts of my heart that need healing and wholeness. I trust that You are a safe place for my most vulnerable truths. Make the mirror a meeting place between my brokenness and Your grace. In Jesus' name, Amen.

Journal Notes:

Journal Notes:

Day 38:

Surrendering the Scarcity Story

Scripture:

"I have come that they may have life, and have it to the full."—John 10:10 b (NIV)

Devotional Reflection:

Scarcity doesn't just live in your wallet, it lives in your mind, your relationships, your dreams. It convinces you that there's not enough love, time, joy, opportunity. It tells you to play small, settle early, and expect less. Because if you expect less, you can't be disappointed, right?
Wrong.

Scarcity isn't safety, it's a prison.

Jesus didn't come to give you a life of "barely enough." He came to give you *abundance*. Not just in money or success, but in peace, purpose, freedom, love, and joy that overflows even when circumstances don't cooperate.

But to step into that abundance, you have to stop clinging to lack. You have to silence the voice that says, *"It's too late for you." "There's no space at the table." "You don't deserve more."*

You do.

You are not a second-class daughter. You are not an afterthought. You are not at the back of the line when God's blessings are being handed out.

This solo journey is about *retraining your heart* to expect good from God again. To believe that He is not withholding from you. That He has not forgotten you. That He delights in blessing you.

So, open your hands. Let go of the scarcity story. Stop living like you're an orphan and remember, you're a daughter of the King.

Journal Prompts:

1. What areas of your life have been shaped by a scarcity mindset?

   ____
   ____
   ____
   ____
   ____
   ____

2. Where did you learn to believe that there's "not enough" for you?

   ____
   ____
   ____
   ____
   ____

3. What would it look like to live with open hands and an expectant heart?

Prayer:

Jesus, I've believed the lie that I don't have enough, am not enough, or won't receive enough. But You are my Shepherd, I lack nothing. Help me let go of the scarcity story and step into Your abundance. Teach me to trust that You are not holding out on me. Let my life reflect a faith that expects You to move in beautiful, overflowing ways. In Jesus' name, Amen.

Journal Notes:

Journal Notes:

Day 39:

Walking in Gentle Strength

Scripture:

"The Lord is my strength and my shield; my heart trusts in him, and he helps me. My heart leaps for joy, and with my song I praise him."— Psalm 28:7 (NIV)

Devotional Reflection:

You've spent so long trying to be strong.

Strong for your kids.
Strong for your family.
Strong in the face of disappointment.
Strong when your heart was breaking behind the scenes.

But there's a different kind of strength that God wants to birth in you, gentle strength. Strength that doesn't roar, but rests. Strength that doesn't posture, but surrenders.

Paul begged God to take away his weakness, but God said no, not to punish him, but to show him that power and weakness are not opposites. In the Kingdom, weakness is an invitation for grace to shine.

Gentle strength is not about shrinking back or staying silent when truth must be spoken. It is the courage to stand firm without needing to crush others to do it. It is the ability to show up fully without wearing yourself out trying to prove your worth.

The world teaches that strength is loud, unbending, and constantly on guard. But Jesus showed a different way. His strength looked like compassion for the outcast, patience with the slow-to-believe, mercy toward the undeserving. He could command the winds and waves with a word, yet He also cradled children in His arms and knelt to wash dusty feet.

This is the kind of strength that endures because it's rooted in God's presence, not in your performance. It's the strength of a woman who knows she doesn't have to hold the whole world together, because she is held.

Let God redefine what strength looks like for you. Let Him teach you how to be soft without breaking, firm without fear, open without shame. This is the strength of a woman who trusts the One who shields her, carries her, and fills her with unshakable joy.

Journal Prompts:

1. How have you equated strength with performance or perfection?

   ____
   ____
   ____
   ____
   ____
   ____

2. Where in your life is God inviting you to embrace gentle strength instead of striving?

3. What does His grace want to carry for you today?

Prayer:

Lord, I'm tired of pretending to be strong in my own power. I give You my weaknesses. Teach me to walk in gentle strength, the kind that is rooted in grace and not performance. Let me be bold, not because I have it all together, but because You hold me together. Fill me with a holy confidence that relies fully on You. In Jesus' name, Amen.

Journal Notes:

Journal Notes:

Day 40:

Celebrating Small Beginnings

Scripture:

"Do not despise these small beginnings, for the Lord rejoices to see the work begin."—Zechariah 4:10 a (NLT)

Devotional Reflection:

You may not feel like much is changing.

You may not have a dramatic testimony or a five-step success story.

But here's what you do have, a beginning.

And beginnings are sacred.

Every forest started with a seed. Every healing began with a tear. Every comeback started with one brave, quiet "yes."

We often want the finished product, but God celebrates the process. He rejoices not in the polish, but in the start. When you get up and choose joy, when you pray even when you're tired, when you say "no more" to what once broke you, that is holy ground.

Beginnings often feel small, but small is not insignificant. A mustard seed may fit between your fingertips, yet it holds the potential to grow into something that provides shade and shelter. You may feel like you're barely holding it together, but God sees the greatness in the seed. He sees the ripple effect of your obedience even when you can't.

Small beginnings are where character is formed, faith is strengthened, and trust is refined. They are where you learn to depend on God instead of the applause of people. If you skip the seed stage, you miss the deep roots that will keep you standing when the storms come.

The world may not clap for your small beginnings, but heaven rejoices. Don't rush past the early steps. Don't curse your pace. Don't compare your starting line to someone else's highlight reel. Every mighty move of God begins with obedience in obscurity.

And here's the truth, what feels small to you may be monumental in God's plan. One prayer may shift generations. One step may lead to a miracle. One moment of obedience may open the door for someone else's breakthrough.

So, celebrate. Clap for yourself. Heaven already is. Your beginning is not just the start of something; it's the start of everything.

Journal Prompts:

1. What small but meaningful step have you taken in this season that deserves celebration?

   ____

   ____

2. How can you shift your mindset to value the process and not just the outcome?

3. What would it look like to honor where you are instead of shaming yourself for where you're not?

Prayer:

God, thank You that You don't overlook the small things. Thank You for rejoicing in my beginnings and reminding me that growth often starts quietly. Help me honor the journey instead of rushing the destination. Teach me to see the beauty in every step, every choice, every act of faith. I'm moving forward and You are with me. In Jesus' name, Amen.

Journal Notes:

Day 41:

The Power of Stillness

Scripture:

"The Lord will fight for you; you need only to be still."
—Exodus 14:14 (NIV)

Devotional Reflection:

Stillness is not inactivity. It is not laziness, apathy, or weakness. Stillness is a sacred act of trust, a declaration that you no longer need to strive, scramble, or solve everything on your own. Our world celebrates busyness and speed, stillness becomes an act of rebellion against fear and self-reliance.

When the Israelites stood at the edge of the Red Sea, terrified of the Egyptian army pursuing them, their first instinct was to panic. But God, through Moses, told them something profound: "Be still. Let Me fight for you." That command was not passive. It required great courage to stop running, stop strategizing, and simply trust God to make a way.

On your solo journey, there will be moments when your natural instinct is to act, to fix, to control, to manage. But some of the greatest breakthroughs happen not through your effort, but through your surrender. Stillness invites God into the battle. It allows Him to move in ways your hands cannot. It slows your heart enough to hear His voice and recalibrate your spirit.

Stillness doesn't mean you do nothing; it means you stop doing *everything* out of fear. It means you intentionally quiet the noise and listen for the whisper of God's direction. It means choosing rest, choosing peace, and choosing trust, even when your circumstances scream otherwise.

Stillness also offers you a chance to see clearly. When you cease the striving, you begin to discern what is truly urgent versus what is noise. You begin to notice what your soul has been trying to say underneath the hustle. You realize that God has been speaking all along, but your pace made it hard to hear.

Being still is a radical act of worship. It's saying, "God, I don't have to work myself into exhaustion to prove my worth. I trust You to be God while I rest in Your presence." That kind of stillness is not just restful, it's transformative.

Journal Prompts:

1. Where in your life have you been striving instead of surrendering?

   ____
   ____
   ____
   ____
   ____
   ____

2. What fears have been keeping you from embracing stillness?

   ____
   ____
   ____
   ____

3. How can you intentionally create space today to be still before God?

Prayer:

God, You see my heart, anxious and always busy. Teach me to be still. Quiet the noise around me and within me so I can sense Your presence and trust Your power. Remind me that I don't have to fight every battle, You are already fighting on my behalf. Today, I choose to release control and rest in Your capable hands. In Jesus' name, Amen.

Journal Notes:

Journal Notes:

Day 42:

Confronting the Lie of Inadequacy

Scripture:

"Not that we are competent in ourselves to claim anything for ourselves, but our competence comes from God."
—2 Corinthians 3:5 (NIV)

Devotional Reflection:

Inadequacy is a thief. It sneaks into your soul, often disguised as humility, and begins to chip away at your confidence. It whispers that you are not equipped, not smart enough, not strong enough. And over time, if left unchecked, it becomes a belief system that informs every decision you make.

We often look at others and assume they have it all together. We compare our internal battles to their external successes and quietly disqualify ourselves from the race. But God never intended for you to live under the shadow of inadequacy. He never called you to measure yourself by the world's impossible standards. Your value is not in what you accomplish, but in *whose* you are.

When Paul wrote that our competence comes from God, he was reminding us that we are not meant to be self-sufficient. In fact, self-sufficiency can be a barrier to grace. When we insist on proving ourselves, we cut ourselves off from the divine help that is available to us. Our culture celebrates "doing it all" and "being enough on our own," but God celebrates dependence on Him.

You were never meant to carry the weight of your purpose without divine help. God doesn't expect you to have it all together, He wants to walk with you, equip you, and empower you for what He has called you to do. Every time you feel inadequate, that is an opportunity to lean deeper into His sufficiency.

On this solo journey, you must confront the lie of inadequacy head-on. You must recognize it as a tactic of the enemy to keep you small, silent, and stuck. Because when you believe you're not enough, you stop showing up. You stop dreaming. You stop saying yes to God.

But what if your perceived inadequacies are actually where God wants to show up the most? What if the very place you feel unqualified is where His power wants to flow?

Your weakness does not disqualify you. It qualifies you for grace. So, stop shrinking. Stop apologizing for your existence. You are already enough because God is more than enough in you.

Journal Prompts:

1. What is one area of your life where you feel most inadequate?

   ____
   ____
   ____
   ____

2. How has that belief affected the way you show up or hold back?

3. What truth from God's Word can you begin to replace that lie with?

Prayer:

Lord, I confess that I have believed I am not enough. I have allowed fear and comparison to keep me from fully walking in my purpose. But today, I choose to reject the lie of inadequacy. I believe that my competence comes from You. Fill every gap in me with Your grace. Help me walk boldly in the truth of who I am in You. In Jesus' name, Amen.

Journal Notes:

Day 43:

Permission to Let Go

Scripture:

"Cast your cares on the Lord and He will sustain you; He will never let the righteous be shaken." —Psalms 55:22 (NIV)

Devotional Reflection:

Letting go can feel like betrayal, betrayal of your memories, your love, your past self. But the truth is, letting go is not forgetting, it's freeing. It's recognizing that the chapter may have ended, but your story is still being written, and God holds the pen.

There is a difference between remembering and dwelling. Memory honors the past; dwelling binds you to it. When you dwell in a place God has called you out of, you keep your feet stuck in yesterday's soil and forfeit the fresh ground He is preparing for you today.

Sometimes we hold on because the pain feels familiar. Even when it's heavy, it's predictable. We think, If I keep replaying the hurt, maybe I can make sense of it. But the truth is, God isn't asking you to make sense of what He's already decided to redeem. He's asking you to trust that the ending you feared is not the ending He's writing.

Letting go means trusting that God can use every broken piece for something beautiful, even when you can't yet see the mosaic. It means giving yourself permission to cry when memories surface but refusing to chain yourself to them. It's choosing to believe that His "next" for you will be far greater than your "was."

And here's the beautiful thing: letting go does not mean you are heartless. It means you are courageous enough to release what was never meant to be your permanent dwelling. It's saying, "Lord, I trust You more than I trust my own grip."

Jesus Himself modeled letting go of His own will in the Garden of Gethsemane, of the crowds who misunderstood Him, of the pain He endured on the cross. And every release led to resurrection. The same will be true for you.

You are not abandoning your past, you are rising from it. And every step forward is proof that you have chosen healing over history.

Journal Prompts:

1. What are you still holding on to that God may be asking you to release?

   ____

   ____

   ____

   ____

   ____

   ____

2. How has dwelling on the past kept you from moving forward?

   ____

   ____

3. What would it feel like to truly believe God is doing something new in your life?

Prayer:

God, I release the past into Your hands. I surrender the people, the memories, and the regrets that have kept me stuck. Help me to trust that letting go is not losing, it is creating space for the new. I open my hands to receive what You are doing now. Make a way in my wilderness, and rivers in my desert. In Jesus' name, Amen.

Journal Notes:

Journal Notes:

Day 44:

Embracing Emotional Honesty

Scripture:

"Trust in Him at all times, you people; pour out your hearts to Him, for God is our refuge." —Psalm 62:8 (NIV)

Devotional Reflection:

We have been taught to be strong. To hold it together. To smile through pain and press on. But emotional suppression is not strength; it's survival. And God didn't call you to merely survive. He called you to live fully, honestly, and healed.

Emotional honesty is a spiritual discipline. It is an act of faith that says, "God, You are safe enough for my truth." When you are honest about where you are, you create space for God to meet you there—not in the place you pretend to be.

We often think strength means presenting our best face to the world, but that kind of strength is brittle; it cracks under pressure. Real strength is rooted in authenticity. It is the courage to say, "I'm not okay right now, but I'm still trusting God."

God doesn't bless the mask; He blesses the person underneath it. He is not impressed by our ability to hold it together. He is moved by our willingness to open our hearts wide, even when they feel messy, raw, or unpresentable.

There is power in naming your feelings. When you say, "God, I'm angry. I'm scared. I'm tired," you're not dishonoring Him, you're honoring the relationship. You're showing that you trust Him enough to see you unfiltered. That is intimacy. That is worship.

David did it in the Psalms, sometimes praising, sometimes lamenting, sometimes asking why. Jeremiah poured out his grief. Even Jesus wept openly and wrestled with His anguish in Gethsemane. If the Son of God could bring His unvarnished heart to the Father, so can you.

Emotional honesty doesn't weaken your witness; it deepens it. It frees you from performance and draws you into alignment with the God who already knows your heart. It gives others permission to be real, too.

So, stop apologizing for your emotions. Stop editing your prayers to make them "acceptable." God can handle your heartbreak. He can sit with your silence. He can hold your tears. And in your honesty, you'll find His comfort rushes in like a flood.

Your vulnerability is not a burden, it's a bridge. It's where your humanity meets His divinity, and where healing begins.

Journal Prompts:

1. What emotions have you been hiding, even from yourself?

   ____

   ____

   ____

   ____

2. What do you fear will happen if you let yourself fully feel?

3. How can you begin to bring your unfiltered heart before God?

Prayer:

Lord, I have tried to be strong for too long. I have hidden my emotions out of fear, shame, or survival. Today, I bring my whole heart to You, the joy, the sorrow, the confusion, the hope. Meet me in my raw places. Be my refuge and my release. Let my honesty be the path to my healing. In Jesus' name, Amen.

Journal Notes:

Day 45:

One Step at a Time

Scripture:

"The path of the righteous is like the morning sun, shining ever brighter till the full light of day."— Proverbs 4:18 (NIV)

Devotional Reflection:

Becoming is not a single leap, it's a lifetime of small, faithful steps. It's not about waking up one morning fully transformed, but about showing up day after day, aligning your steps with God's truth until you look back and realize you are living in a light you once only imagined.

The woman you dream of being, confident, healed, anchored in faith, already exists inside you. She's not waiting to be "found"; she's being revealed. Every prayer you pray, every lie you replace with God's truth, every act of obedience when no one is watching these are the bricks being laid on the path toward her.

She is not born in grand, flashy moments. She is formed in the hidden places:

- In your quiet choice to forgive when it would be easier to stay bitter.
- In your decision to rest instead of endlessly proving your worth.

- In your whisper to God for strength when you feel like giving up.
- In the gentle way you now speak to yourself, replacing self-criticism with compassion.

The truth is, some days will feel slow. Some steps will feel small. And some seasons will make you wonder if you're even moving at all. But progress in God's kingdom is rarely loud, it's steady. And every step forward, no matter how tiny, is a victory that Heaven sees.

God isn't rushing you. He's not impatient with your pace. The same God who authored your beginning is already holding your ending, and He is faithful to complete the work He started in you. Every tear you've cried, every moment you've doubted, every prayer you've whispered in exhaustion, He has counted and collected them all.

So today, take the step. Just one. Even if it feels small. Even if it feels unseen. Because in God's hands, every step builds into something eternal. You are not who you were yesterday, and you are not yet who you will be tomorrow. Right here, right now, you are beautifully becoming.

Journal Prompts:

1. Who is the woman God is shaping you into?

____

____

____

____

____

____

2. What evidence do you see of His work in you, even if it feels small?

____

____

____

____

____

____

3. What promise from God can you cling to as you continue your journey?

____

____

____

____

____

____

Prayer:

God, thank You for the work You are doing in me. Even when I feel stuck or slow, I trust that You are moving. Help me see myself through Your eyes, in process, on purpose, and filled with potential. I believe that the good work You started in me, You will finish. I am becoming. And I trust You with the journey. In Jesus' name, Amen.

Journal Notes:

Day 46:

Restoring the Ruins

Scripture:

"Come, let us rebuild the wall of Jerusalem, and we will no longer be in disgrace." —Nehemiah 2:17 (NIV)

Devotional Reflection:

Every setback leaves rubble, shattered dreams, fractured trust, plans that seem beyond repair. Like Jerusalem's broken walls, your life may bear scars of seasons where everything collapsed. Yet ruins are not the end of the story; they are the canvas for redemption.

When Nehemiah surveyed Jerusalem, he refused to accept perpetual ruin. He prayed, planned, and partnered with God to rebuild. The work was exhausting, surrounded by opposition, but every stone reset declared, *"Disgrace will not have the last word."*

Your ruin might look like a failed relationship, a lost job, or a hidden habit that cost you dearly. But God specializes in restoration. He collects the scattered stones of your past mistakes, regrets, forgotten callings and invites you to rebuild with Him. Restoring isn't about returning to what was; it's about constructing something stronger, wiser, and rooted in grace.

Rebuilding requires honesty about the damage, courage to begin, and perseverance when opposition resurfaces. Yet each repaired gap proclaims God's faithfulness: what shame tried to bury, grace will resurrect. Don't fear the rubble, see it as raw material. Together with God, you'll raise walls that testify to hope.

Sometimes rebuilding begins before anything looks different. It starts with the decision to believe again, to forgive, to dream, and to rise when it's easier to stay buried in brokenness. Healing doesn't always look like the life you had before; often, it looks like something entirely new. But that newness holds greater strength because it has been refined by fire and shaped by God's hands.

There will be moments when fatigue threatens to stop your progress, when critics question your worth, and when old wounds whisper lies. But remember: Nehemiah didn't rebuild the wall alone. God surrounded him with workers, watchers, and warriors. The same God who gave him strength and strategy will do the same for you.

Even in seasons when progress is slow or unseen, trust that God is rebuilding not just what you lost, but who you are. He is restoring your identity, your hope, and your future. And when the wall rises again, it won't be to your glory, but to His.

Journal Prompts:

1. Identify an area of your life that feels like a pile of ruins. What "stones" need picking up first?

   ____

   ____

   ____

2. Where do you notice God prompting you to rebuild instead of retreat?

3. What practical first step can you take this week toward restoration?

Prayer:

Master Builder, stand with me amid my rubble. Give me eyes to see possibility where I only saw disgrace. Strengthen my hands for the work, surround me with encouragers, and rebuild my life stone by stone until it reflects Your glory. Remind me that no ruin is too far gone for Your redemption. In Jesus' name, Amen.

Journal Notes:

Day 47:

The Oil of Intimacy

Scripture:

"The wise ones, however, took oil in jars along with their lamps." —Matthew 25:4 (NIV)

Devotional Reflection:

The parable of the ten virgins reminds us that outward readiness is meaningless without inward reserve. The wise carried extra oil, symbolic of cultivated intimacy with God, so their lamps could burn through the night.

On your solo journey, public light can't outlast private neglect. You may serve, inspire, and achieve, but if intimacy with Jesus dries up, the flame dims. Oil is gathered in secret through whispered prayers, unhurried scripture, silent awe. It's produced when you choose worship over worry, stillness over scrolls, depth over display.

This oil can't be borrowed last minute; it's accrued drop by drop. It sustains you when doors seem delayed, when darkness lingers longer than expected. It keeps hope flickering until the moment answers emerge, break-throughs manifest, or Christ returns.

Guard your reserve. Let intimacy be priority, not afterthought. Your hidden life determines the brilliance of your public witness. Carry extra oil, and your lamp will not sputter but blaze.

The wise virgins didn't wait for crisis to tend to their spiritual well. They prepared in advance, knowing the night would stretch long. In your own life, the waiting seasons, those where prayers seem unanswered and direction feels unclear, will test your oil levels. In those times, it is what you stored in hiddenness that will carry you through.

Extra oil means creating margin in your schedule to hear God's voice. It means tending to your soul when no one is watching. It means becoming a woman who doesn't just know about God but walks with Him daily. When your life is fueled by that kind of intimacy, you will shine even in the darkest nights, and your light will draw others to the Source.

Don't just prepare for moments, prepare for endurance. Let your oil be a steady river, not a last-minute scramble. The deeper your well, the longer your flame can burn.

Journal Prompts:

1. How full is your "oil jar" right now? What activities refill or drain it?

   ____

   ____

   ____

   ____

   ____

   ____

2. What practices can you incorporate daily to deepen intimacy with God?

____

____

____

____

____

____

3. Recall a season when hidden devotion sustained you. What did you learn?

____

____

____

____

____

____

Prayer:

Holy Spirit, fill my jar again. Forgive me for relying on old oil or borrowed fire. Teach me to seek You in quiet corners to delight in Your presence more than platforms. Keep my lamp burning bright until the day I see You face to face. Make my hidden life rich with Your presence so I may walk in power, humility, and steady endurance. In Jesus' name, Amen.

Journal Notes:

Day 48:

Breakthrough

Scripture:

"Humble yourselves, therefore, under God's mighty hand, that He may lift you up in due time." —1 Peter 5:6 (NIV)

Devotional Reflection:

Breakthrough doesn't always begin with a shout. Sometimes, it begins with a bow.

In a culture obsessed with platform, applause, and achievement, humility can feel like weakness. But in the Kingdom of God, humility is the posture that unlocks promotion. It is not thinking less of yourself, it's thinking of yourself rightly: fully dependent on God, surrendered to His timing, and open to His refinement.

On your solo journey, there will be seasons where God gently invites you to *kneel* before you *rise.* Seasons where pride must be stripped, control surrendered, and the illusion of self-sufficiency dismantled. It won't always feel good, but it will be good *for* you.

God doesn't humble to humiliate; He humbles to *heal.* To clear the clutter that blocks His movement in your life. To strip away ego so you can walk in authentic authority. To ensure that when you are elevated, your character can sustain your calling.

Humbling yourself under God's mighty hand is an act of trust. It says, "I don't have to force this. I don't have to prove my worth. I don't need to strive to be seen. God sees me. And He will lift me when the time is right."

Sometimes bowing means confessing when you're wrong. Sometimes it means letting go of being right, letting go of being first, or letting go of being in control. It might mean serving when no one is watching, forgiving before you receive an apology, or obeying when you don't understand the outcome.

But the beauty is this: when you choose humility, God chooses honor. When you kneel in private, He elevates you in ways that no man or platform ever could.

Your breakthrough is not delayed; it's being cultivated through your surrender.

Journal Prompts:

1. In what area of your life is God inviting you to release pride and choose humility?

   ____

   ____

   ____

   ____

   ____

   ____

2. How have you seen surrender lead to breakthrough in the past?

   ____

   ____

   ____

3. What fears arise when you think about bowing before God in this season?

Prayer:

Father, help me to bow before You, not out of fear, but out of faith. Teach me to trust Your timing, Your process, and Your hand. Strip away pride and self-reliance and grow in me a heart that delights in humility. I choose to kneel, knowing You will lift me in due season. Shape my spirit, steady my steps, and let every breakthrough be birthed from surrender. In Jesus' name, Amen.

Journal Notes:

Journal Notes:

Day 49:

Trusting God in the Fog

Scripture:

"Your word is a lamp for my feet, a light on my path."

—Psalm 119:105 (NIV)

Devotional Reflection:

Fog distorts distance. It blurs the familiar landscape and swallows familiar landmarks until even the next few steps feel uncertain. In life's fog seasons when a diagnosis is pending, a job transition looms, or a relationship's future is unclear, clarity feels cruelly scarce. Yet God does not leave you without guidance; He offers a *lamp*, not a *floodlight*.

A lamp illuminates enough for *one* faithful step. It forces dependence, slows frantic pacing, and invites intimacy. Abraham followed God to "a land I will show you" without GPS coordinates. Peter stepped out of a boat onto water with visibility no farther than Christ's outstretched hand. The saints did not see the whole road; they trusted the One who paved it.

Fog is not the failure of God's presence but the forging of your trust. It exposes the illusion that control equals safety, teaching you to trade certainty for confidence in God's character. Each obedient step taken in dim light expands your history with Him proving that even when you could not see, He could.

But trust doesn't mean numbness; it often includes trembling. You can be afraid and still faithful. You can walk with a lump in your throat and still be obedient. It's in the fog that your spiritual muscles are trained, where worship becomes warfare and tears become prayers. Faith, in its purest form, is forged not when everything is clear but when you walk forward anyway.

The fog reminds you that you were never meant to navigate life by sight alone. You were designed to follow the sound of His voice, to let His promises echo louder than the questions in your mind. In those moments, the lamp becomes more than guidance, it becomes comfort. A reminder that even in obscurity, you are seen. Even in silence, you are heard. Even in confusion, you are led.

So, lean into the fog, not with fear, but with reverence. The Holy Spirit often speaks clearest when everything else is quiet. And when clarity comes, you'll look back and see that you were never walking alone. The same God who led you into the unknown was already preparing the next breakthrough just beyond the veil.

When the path is hidden, lean closer to the Guide. Hide His Word in your heart; let its promises glow like embers against the haze. Remember past deliverances, they are compass points. Speak gratitude aloud; it tunes your spirit to the frequency of hope. And rest: fog eventually lifts. Dawn always breaks. Until then, the lamp is enough, and so is the One who holds it.

Journal Prompts:

1. Identify an area of your life currently "in the fog." What emotions surface as you navigate this uncertainty?

____

____

____

____

____

____

2. Recall a past season where God guided you step by step. How does that memory bolster your faith now?

____

____

____

____

____

____

3. What is the single next right step you sense God asking you to take, even without full visibility?

____

____

____

____

____

____

Prayer:

Guide of my journey, I surrender my demand for complete maps. Illuminate my next step and steady my anxious heart.

Remind me that Your presence in the fog is safer than my certainty without You. I choose to walk by the lamp of Your Word, trusting that dawn will break in Your perfect time. In Jesus' name, Amen.

Journal Notes:

Journal Notes:

Day 50:

Living From Overflow

Scripture:

"Whoever believes in Me, as Scripture has said, rivers of living water will flow from within them."
—John 7:38 (NIV)

Devotional Reflection:

God never intended for you to limp through life on spiritual fumes. Jesus envisions you as a riverbed, banks carved out by grace, filled and refilled by the ever-fresh current of the Holy Spirit. Survival *sips* just enough to get by, but overflow *pours*, spilling life wherever it moves.

Overflow begins with abiding. It is the natural outflow of a heart consistently connected to the Source. You cannot manufacture living water; you *host* it. When you dwell in God's presence, He saturates the dry, cracked places of your soul until refreshment becomes your default posture.

Notice, rivers must stay clear to keep flowing. Debris of bitterness, fear, or unconfessed sin can dam the current, reducing vibrant waters to a stagnant pool. Regular repentance keeps channels open. Rhythms of rest, worship, and Scripture meditation widen the riverbanks, increasing capacity for more of Him.

Overflow is not self-indulgent; it is missional. Rivers move toward need. From the overflow of your heart, encouragement becomes instinct, generosity becomes joy, forgiveness becomes possible. Ministry shifts from draining obligation to effortless extension of what God is already doing within. And overflow protects you, it anchors your identity in the Source, not the outcome. You serve not to prove, but because you are already full. You pour not to be praised, but because you've been so deeply filled that silence or selfishness feels unnatural.

Check your source before you check your schedule. Prioritize the secret place over public platforms. Protect margins that allow replenishing practices, lingering prayer walks, device-free Sabbaths, spontaneous worship. As you stay under the fountain, the river will keep running, and desert places around you will bloom.

Overflow is also a safeguard. When you minister from fullness, you're less susceptible to burnout, resentment, or comparison. The world applauds performance, but heaven values presence. God is not impressed by how much you do if your heart is dry in the process. He would rather fill one surrendered soul than watch ten exhausted ones strive for applause.

When you live from overflow, you begin to recognize the sacred in the simple. A conversation becomes a moment of ministry. A shared meal turns into communion. Your presence carries peace, not because of who you are, but because of Who is flowing through you.

Overflow is what transforms survival into significance. It's the difference between barely getting by and powerfully giving out. And the beauty is, it's never something you have to manufacture. Just remain in Him. Just drink deeply. Just show up, open, and yielded. The river knows where to go.

So let go of spiritual scarcity. You were made for more than fragments and fatigue. You were made to overflow, to be filled so continually by the Spirit that your very life becomes a stream of renewal for the world around you.

Journal Prompts:

1. In which areas have you been operating on fumes rather than overflow?

   ____

   ____

   ____

   ____

   ____

   ____

2. What “debris” might be clogging your spiritual river, and how will you address it?

   ____

   ____

   ____

   ____

   ____

   ____

3. Describe a practical rhythm you can adopt this week to remain connected to the Source.

   ____

   ____

   ____

   ____

   ____

   ____

Prayer:

Jesus, immerse me in Your living water until every dry corner of my soul is revived. Expose and clear away blockages of fear, fatigue, or sin. Teach me to remain in You so that Your life can surge through me, refreshing others as I stay continually filled. Make overflow my normal. In Jesus' name, Amen.

Journal Notes:

Journal Notes:

Day 51:

When Obedience Feels Costly

Scripture:

"Sacrifice and offering you did not desire, but my ears you have opened— burnt offerings and sin offerings you did not require. Then I said, 'Here I am, I have come... I desire to do your will, my God.'" —Psalm 40:6–8 (NIV)

Devotional Reflection:

Obedience is often romanticized, but in real life it can feel like a slow surrender, a letting go of what is familiar, safe, or even deeply cherished. Sometimes, obedience doesn't come with applause or immediate clarity. It feels more like a quiet yes in a dimly lit room, a choice that costs you comfort, visibility, or control.

David's words remind us that God isn't impressed by religious performance. He isn't wooed by empty sacrifice. He wants *you*. Your availability. Your yielded heart. Your listening ear. Obedience is birthed not from striving but from surrender, a soul saying, "Here I am, Lord."

On your solo journey, you may be called to obey in ways that stretch your soul. Perhaps it's forgiving someone who doesn't deserve it, walking away from something good to pursue something God, or stepping into a role that feels far beyond your qualifications. It may even mean staying when you want to run or resting when hustle feels holier.

The beauty is this: God doesn't ask for blind obedience. He leads with love and confirms with peace. And every time you say yes, even with trembling hands and tear-streaked prayers, He meets you with provision, assurance, and grace. He's not looking for perfection, just a heart willing to follow.

Obedience isn't about outcome; it's about alignment. When your heart aligns with His will, you'll begin to see fruit even in barren seasons. What feels like loss on the front end often turns out to be the fertile ground of legacy.

You won't always understand the "why" on this side of eternity. But obedience places you in the flow of His favor. You walk under open heavens. You step into divine setups. And as your yes echoes in heaven, breakthrough begins to echo back.

Journal Prompts:

1. What recent invitation to obedience has felt particularly costly?

   ____

   ____

   ____

2. How do you discern the difference between obligation and true obedience?

   ____

   ____

   ____

3. What are you afraid obedience might "cost" you, and what might it *gain* you in God's hands?

Prayer:

Father, open my ears to Your voice and my heart to Your will. Even when I don't fully understand, give me the courage to obey. Strip away performance and fear so that I can say, "Here I am," with full surrender. Let obedience be my act of worship, my love song to You. In Jesus' name, Amen.

Journal Notes:

Journal Notes:

Day 52:

You Are Not Behind

Scripture:

"The Lord is not slow in keeping His promise, as some understand slowness. Instead He is patient with you..."
—2 Peter 3:9 (NIV)

Devotional Reflection:

There's a quiet panic that creeps in when you feel like you're falling behind, behind in your career, relationships, healing, or purpose. You look around and see others "moving forward," and suddenly, your progress feels too slow. You start measuring your worth by the pace of your progress and questioning if you missed your moment.

But God is not watching a clock, He's writing a masterpiece.

Your timeline isn't broken; it's being rebuilt. God is not delayed, distracted, or disappointed. He is intentional. There are sacred lessons hidden in the slower seasons, moments when your roots grow deep, your faith matures, and your vision becomes clear. You are not late; you are being aligned.

The lie that says you're "too late" often comes from comparison, measuring your chapter three against someone else's chapter twenty. But God does not compare you to others. He calls you to walk with Him, not to race against them. And the pace He sets is designed for your refinement, not your punishment.

There is purpose in the pause. There is wisdom in the waiting. Sometimes God places you in divine stillness so He can unearth what busyness kept buried, old mindsets, insecurities, unhealed wounds, or even misplaced desires. Slower seasons aren't wasted seasons; they are often the ones that define the depth of your trust.

Remember: Jesus raised Lazarus four days late by human standards, but perfectly on time by divine design. Sometimes, what feels like delay is actually preparation. Sometimes, what feels like falling behind is God slowing you down so He can walk beside you more intimately.

You don't have to prove anything. You don't have to catch up. You just have to keep going, with grace, with faith, and with the assurance that your pace is not a reflection of your worth. Stop rushing healing. Stop comparing your journey. You are not in a race; you are on a path. And that path is curated by the God who knows you, sees you, and leads you, not according to the world's schedule but by the rhythm of grace.

Breathe. Rest. Reset. Trust that you are exactly where you need to be for who God is calling you to become. Not late. Not lost. Just deeply loved and divinely led.

Journal Prompts:

1. In what area of your life have you felt "behind"? Why?

   ____

   ____

   ____

   ____

   ____

2. How have you seen God's timing work out in your favor before?

3. What would it look like to trust that you are *right on time*?

Prayer:

Father, help me silence the pressure to perform or catch up. Remind me that I am on Your timeline, not the world's. Teach me to embrace the pace You've set for me, to trust Your timing, and to rest in the truth that I have not missed anything You've ordained for me. In Jesus' name, Amen.

Journal Notes:

Day 53:

Permission to Begin Again

Scripture:

"Brothers and sisters, I do not consider myself yet to have taken hold of it. But one thing I do: Forgetting what is behind and straining toward what is ahead, 14I press on toward the goal to win the prize for which God has called me heavenward in Christ Jesus."—Philippians 3:13-14 (NIV)

Devotional Reflection:

Sometimes the bravest thing you can do is start again, when the dream failed, when the relationship broke, when the version of yourself you once celebrated no longer fits. The temptation is to cling to the old, trying to salvage something from the rubble. But God doesn't just repair; He renews.

You have permission to begin again. Not because you have all the answers, but because God is already doing something new within you.

Beginning again is not a sign of failure; it's a sign of faith. Faith to believe there's more ahead than behind. Faith to walk away from what no longer aligns with who you're becoming. Faith to release the guilt, shame, or pressure that tells you it's "too late."

Every new beginning requires a holy goodbye. You may grieve what was, but you don't have to be chained to it. God is not defined by your past decisions, and neither are you. You are evolving, unfolding, becoming more of who He originally designed.

It takes courage to close a chapter without a clear outline for the next one. It takes surrender to trust that the same God who met you in the old place will meet you again in this new one. Starting over doesn't mean you lost. It means you've learned. It means you've been refined by fire and are now ready to rise.

Beginnings are sacred. They hold whispers of redemption and glimpses of glory. And though they often come dressed in uncertainty, they are filled with divine possibilities. You are not just circling back; you are spiraling upward. This is not the same starting line. You're wiser now. Softer. Stronger. And far more equipped.

So don't shrink. Don't apologize for outgrowing what once fit. Don't fear the blank page. The Author of your life hasn't put down His pen.

Start again with wonder. Start again with courage. Let go of what didn't work and lean into what is waiting. There is beauty in fresh starts, and God delights in doing a new thing, even in the ashes.

Journal Prompts:

1. What is something you need to release so you can begin again?

   ____

   ____

   ____

   ____

2. How have you seen God give you a new beginning in the past?

3. What would "starting fresh" look like in your current season?

Prayer:

God, thank You for new beginnings. Help me release the fear and shame that keep me stuck in the past. Show me the next faithful step toward the future You're preparing. Give me strength to begin again, this time with You at the center. In Jesus' name, Amen.

Journal Notes:

Day 54:

Becoming Her Takes Time

Scripture:

"Let perseverance finish its work so that you may be mature and complete, not lacking anything."— James 1:4 (NIV)

Devotional Reflection:

The version of you becoming the one who walks confidently, loves freely, lives authentically; that version doesn't emerge overnight. She is formed through time, trials, truth, and trust. Becoming is a process, not an event.

Culture celebrates quick transformations: glow-ups, break-throughs, and overnight success. But in God's kingdom, the process is the point. He is just as present in your "becoming" as He is in your becoming "her."

Don't despise the messy middle. That's where the soil of your soul is turned, pruned, and fertilized for growth. It's where God rewrites old stories, dismantles lies, and heals hidden wounds. Becoming slow because it is sacred. Rushing it would be like picking fruit before it's ripe, still full of potential, but not yet sweet.

There's no shame in still becoming. No guilt in needing grace. You don't have to arrive to be worthy of love, belonging, or purpose. You are not less holy in your healing. You are not less valuable in your vulnerability. Becoming her takes time, but you're not doing it alone.

God is not in a hurry. He is a Master Builder, patient, precise, and deeply personal. And He promises to finish what He started.

And while you're waiting, He's working. Every detour, every delay, every moment that feels like a setback is actually an invitation to deeper surrender. You're not "behind", you're being built brick by brick, layer by layer. The woman you admire, the version of you that reflects wholeness and boldness, she didn't emerge fully formed. She was developed in the hidden places where only God could see.

Let the process tenderize you. Let it teach you how to rest without rushing, how to grow without grasping, how to stand in purpose even while still healing. Your becoming isn't a countdown to perfection; it's a daily unveiling of who you've always been in God's eyes.

The transformation is already happening. Trust the slow work of grace.

Journal Prompts:

1. What parts of "her", your ideal self are already showing up in your life?

   ____
   ____
   ____
   ____
   ____

2. Where do you feel tempted to rush your healing or growth?

3. How can you be more patient with your own process?

Prayer:

Father, thank You for being patient with me as I grow. Help me trust Your timing and surrender my need to arrive quickly. Teach me to honor the process, to embrace where I am today, and to believe that You are faithfully completing the work You began in me. In Jesus' name, Amen.

Journal Notes:

Day 55:

What You Carry Matters

Scripture:

"Cast all your anxiety on Him because He cares for you."
—1 Peter 5:7 (NIV)

Devotional Reflection:

There are things you were never meant to carry, guilt, shame, people's expectations, and unresolved pain. Yet on this journey, you may find yourself lugging around emotional baggage that weighs down your spirit and clouds your vision. Often, we become so used to the weight that we forget what it feels like to be free. We call it "being strong," when in truth, it's a form of silent suffering. We press forward with smiles while our hearts are quietly breaking under burdens God never asked us to hold.

But God invites you to release it. To place the heaviness in His hands and walk forward unburdened. The cross wasn't just about forgiveness of sin, it was about freedom from oppression, deliverance from bondage, and healing for the soul. Jesus didn't die so you could survive weighted down. He rose so you could walk in resurrection life, light, unchained, and whole.

Letting go is an act of trust. It's a declaration that God can handle what you cannot. You weren't created to carry everything; you were created to cast it on Him. Even the silent burdens, the secret battles, and the pain you never put words to,

He sees it all, and He welcomes it. He doesn't call you weak for laying it down; He calls you wise.

And here's the truth: what you carry matters, because it shapes how you show up in the world. Carrying bitterness filters how you see people. Carrying guilt distorts your view of grace. Carrying fear hinders how freely you love. Sometimes, the bravest thing you can do isn't pushing through, but pausing to unpack what's too heavy for your soul.

Ask yourself: What have I normalized that is no longer mine to carry? Who or what am I still holding onto that God has asked me to release?

You are not more righteous by holding it all together. You are not more spiritual by pretending you're fine. The lighter you walk, the freer you become. And freedom is where healing begins, not at the finish line, but at the moment of surrender.

Journal Prompts:

1. What am I carrying that is no longer mine to hold?

   ____

   ____

   ____

   ____

   ____

   ____

2. What would it look like to fully surrender that burden to God?

   ____

   ____

   ____

3. How does carrying too much effect my peace, relationships, or purpose?

Prayer:

God, show me what I've been carrying that You never asked me to bear. Teach me to release the weight and trust You with the pieces I can't fix. Remind me that I was never meant to journey alone or burdened. Thank You for caring enough to carry it all. In Jesus' name, Amen.

Journal Notes:

Journal Notes:

Day 56:

The Power of Saying No

Scripture:

"All you need to say is simply 'Yes' or 'No'; anything beyond this comes from the evil one."—Matthew 5:37 (NIV)

Devotional Reflection:

On this solo journey, one of the most powerful tools you have is your "no." Not a reactive or bitter no, but a sacred, Spirit-led no that protects your peace, honors your boundaries, and keeps your heart aligned with your purpose. It's the kind of no that comes from a woman who knows who she is, whose she is, and where she's going.

Your "no" is not selfish, it's stewardship. It means you are taking ownership of the limited energy, time, and space you've been given and choosing to invest it wisely. Saying no is not rejection, it's redirection. It's a declaration that your time, energy, and calling are not for sale. That not every opportunity is yours to chase. That you are no longer bending and breaking to please others at the expense of your own well-being.

In a world that praises busyness and celebrates saying yes to everything, learning to say no can feel countercultural. But Jesus modeled this beautifully. He withdrew from the crowds. He chose solitude. He didn't meet every demand or respond to every need. He lived with a holy focus, listening for the Father's voice and doing only what He saw the Father doing.

Likewise, you don't have to explain or apologize for walking in discernment. Every yes has a cost and sometimes, your peace, your purpose, and your rest are too expensive to trade. The more you grow, the more intentional your yes must become.

God never asked you to be everything to everyone. He asked you to be faithful to what He's assigned you. And sometimes faithfulness looks like rest. Sometimes obedience looks like turning things down. Sometimes it looks like choosing the slower, quieter path that aligns with your soul rather than the loud, attention-grabbing road of people-pleasing.

Your "no" sets you free to live from a place of conviction, not comparison. It sets boundaries that keep the wrong things out and make room for the right things to grow. It's how you guard your heart, protect your purpose, and walk in wisdom.

Remember this: every "no" to what's not aligned is a "yes" to God's best. And that kind of obedience firm, quiet, Spirit-led is powerful beyond words.

Journal Prompts:

1. Where in my life have I been afraid to say no?

   ____

   ____

   ____

   ____

   ____

   ____

2. How can setting boundaries protect what God is building in me?

3. What is one thing I need to say "no" to this week?

Prayer:

God, give me the courage to say no without guilt and yes without fear. Help me honor what You're doing in me by protecting the space where growth happens. Let my boundaries be blessed, not burdensome. Teach me to say no from a place of wisdom and peace. In Jesus' name, Amen.

Journal Notes:

Journal Notes:

Day 57:

Don't Water Down Who You Are

Scripture:

"For we are God's masterpiece. He has created us anew in Christ Jesus, so we can do the good things He planned for us long ago."—Ephesians 2:10 (NLT)

Devotional Reflection:

There's a subtle pressure in the world to shrink, to tone yourself down so others feel comfortable, to dilute your voice so you don't seem "too much," to edit your truth so it doesn't ruffle feathers.

But you weren't created to be a watered-down version of yourself. You are God's masterpiece, vivid, intentional, and deeply valuable. The fullness of who you are is not a flaw to fix, it's a reflection of the divine creativity of your Creator. When God formed you, He didn't make a mistake. He didn't overdo it. He handcrafted you with intention, layering strength and softness, boldness and grace, courage and compassion.

Your voice carries power. Your presence shifts atmospheres. Your story, yes, even the messy, imperfect parts are sacred and necessary. Don't underestimate how your journey speaks life to someone else's valley. The very things you've tried to hide, or silence may be the keys to someone else's freedom.

You were never meant to blend in when you were created to stand out. The enemy would love nothing more than for you to shrink, to dim your light, to quiet your truth, because he knows the damage your authenticity does to darkness. But heaven is cheering you on. God delights in your full expression. He calls you to rise, to speak, to lead, to shine and not in arrogance, but in holy confidence.

Stop apologizing for being who God made you to be. Stop shrinking in spaces you were born to stand tall in. Your boldness is not too much. Your clarity is not intimidating. Your light is not a threat, it's a revelation. Let people adjust to your authenticity or quietly exit your life but never adjust your light to fit in the shadows.

When you walk in your fullness, you give others permission to do the same. You become a living invitation for others to rise. And as you take up space with grace, you become a lighthouse, guiding others back to the truth that they, too, are allowed to shine.

Journal Prompts:

1. Where have I been shrinking or watering myself down to be accepted?

   ____

   ____

   ____

   ____

   ____

   ____

2. What does walking in my full, authentic self look like?

   ____

   ____

3. What would I say, do, or become if I stopped apologizing for who I am?

Prayer:

God, remind me that I am Your masterpiece. Teach me to walk boldly in the fullness of who You created me to be. Silence the voices, internal and external that tell me I need to shrink. Help me embrace the beauty of my design without fear. In Jesus' name, Amen.

Journal Notes:

Journal Notes:

Day 58:

The Silence is Not a Punishment

Scripture:

"Truly my soul finds rest in God; my salvation comes from him. Truly he is my rock and my salvation; he is my fortress, I will never be shaken."—Psalms 62:1-2 (NIV)

Devotional Reflection:

There will be seasons on this solo journey when it feels like heaven has gone quiet. No clear signs. No open doors. No fresh revelation. Just stillness.

But don't confuse silence with absence.

God is not punishing you; He's preparing you. The stillness is not a rejection, it's a recalibration. It's the sacred space where your soul is quieted so you can hear what can't be heard through noise. This silence, though unsettling at times, is holy ground. It's where God develops something deeper than feelings, He births faith.

When we are addicted to constant movement and instant answers, divine stillness can feel uncomfortable. But it's in these quiet places that God invites you to become rooted, not just reactive. The silence is not empty, it is full of His presence, full of unseen work, full of preparation.

This is where you learn the difference between God's hand and His heart. When you can no longer trace His hand, you begin to truly trust His heart. The quiet seasons strip away distractions and teach you to anchor your soul in what is eternal rather than emotional. They test whether your faith is based on signs and outcomes, or on a relationship with the One who never changes.

God is still moving in the silence. He's maturing you. He's rearranging things behind the scenes. He's cultivating a deeper level of intimacy that doesn't rely on performance or proof.

And when He speaks again because He *will*, you'll hear Him more clearly. You'll have ears trained by trust, a heart softened by waiting, and a spirit strong enough to carry what He reveals next.

So, don't rush out of the stillness. Don't resent the silence. Receive it as the sacred hush before your next breakthrough.

Journal Prompts:

1. How do I typically respond when God feels silent?

____

____

____

____

____

____

2. What might God be teaching or developing in this quiet season?

____

____

____

3. What does it look like to trust God even when I don't hear Him?

Prayer:

God, when it feels quiet, help me not to panic. Remind me that Your silence is never abandonment. Strengthen my faith to believe that You are still working behind the scenes. Teach me to rest in Your presence even when I don't have answers. In Jesus' name, Amen.

Journal Notes:

Journal Notes:

Day 59:

Nothing Is Wasted

Scripture:

"And we know that in all things God works for the good of those who love Him, who have been called according to His purpose."—Romans 8:28 (NIV)

Devotional Reflection:

Not the heartbreak. Not the detour. Not the season you thought would kill you. *Nothing* is wasted, not in God's hands.

He is the Master Redeemer, turning ashes into beauty, loss into wisdom, and brokenness into purpose. What feels like the end is often the soil where new life begins. God doesn't discard your pain; He repurposes it. He doesn't gloss over your wounds; He heals them from the inside out and uses them as the very places where His glory can shine through.

Even the moments that broke your heart, stripped you bare, or left you confused are held in His loving hands. Nothing is beyond His reach or outside His plan. The detours you despised; they shaped your endurance. The delays that frustrated you; they developed your character. The rejection that nearly crushed you; it redirected you toward a higher calling.

You may not see it now. You may still be carrying the weight of unanswered questions. But rest assured, God wastes nothing. What you walked through will not only be used to strengthen *you* but will become a bridge of hope for someone else. What looked like a grave was actually a garden in disguise.

Don't let shame silence your story. The enemy wants you to believe your past disqualifies you, but God uses that very past to *qualify* you for the work ahead. Your scars are evidence, not of defeat, but of survival. Of grace. Of God's unwavering faithfulness.

So don't throw away your past. Don't hide the parts you wish never happened. Bring them to God as an offering, broken, raw, and real. He doesn't need perfection. He desires your surrender. And in His hands, even your deepest pain becomes sacred ground for purpose.

What you thought would break you might just be the very thing that builds you.

Journal Prompts:

1. What part of my story have I been trying to forget or hide?

   ____
   ____
   ____
   ____
   ____
   ____

2. How might God use that very part for His glory and my healing?

____
____
____
____
____
____

3. What does it mean to me that "nothing is wasted"?

____
____
____
____
____
____

Prayer:

God, thank You that You waste nothing. Even in the places I feel ashamed or broken, You are able to redeem and repurpose it for good. Teach me to see my past through the lens of grace. Use every part of my journey for Your glory. In Jesus' name, Amen.

Journal Notes:

____
____
____
____

Journal Notes:

Day 60:

You're Still Becoming

Scripture:

"And after you have suffered a little while, the God of all grace, who called you to His eternal glory in Christ, will Himself restore, confirm, strengthen, and establish you."
— 1 Peter 5:10 (ESV)

Devotional Reflection:

You're not behind. You're not broken. You're not too late. *You are still becoming*, and that is *holy.*

The journey is not about perfection, it's about persistence. It's about rising when you fall, showing up when you're weary, and trusting God even when the path feels uncertain. Each step you take, even the shaky, tear-filled ones, is evidence that grace is still carrying you. You may not feel finished, but you are being *faithfully* formed.

Let go of the pressure to arrive. This is not a race to a destination. This is a sacred unfolding. Growth isn't always loud or visible. Sometimes it's silent work, God chiseling your heart in private, strengthening your soul in the hidden places, healing wounds you forgot you had. He's not in a hurry with your process, so why are you?

The enemy wants you to believe that you're too far gone, that you've missed your moment. But the truth is, *you are right on time for your assignment.* God's timing is perfect, and so is His preparation. The delay is not denial; it's development. You are not stuck; you are being *strategically shaped* for where He's taking you.

Celebrate your becoming. Celebrate the woman you're evolving into. The one who's learning to speak with wisdom, to rest without guilt, to pray with boldness, to forgive deeply, and to walk in joy even when the answers don't come quickly.

You're not who you used to be. And you're not yet who you will become. But right here in this middle space, in this beautiful tension of transformation, you are *deeply loved, divinely held,* and *still becoming.*

And that becoming? It's sacred. It's significant. It's a sign that God is not finished with you, He's just getting started.

Journal Prompts:

1. What small ways have I grown over the past few months?

    ____
    ____
    ____
    ____
    ____
    ____

2. How can I celebrate progress instead of focusing on perfection?

    ____
    ____

3. What does "becoming" look like for me right now?

Prayer:

God, thank You for still working in me. Help me be patient with my process and kind to myself as I grow. I surrender to Your timing and trust that You are completing the good work You began in me. Thank You that I'm still becoming, and I don't have to rush it. In Jesus' name, Amen.

Journal Notes:

Journal Notes:

Day 61:

Breaking the Silence

Scripture:

"She gave this name to the Lord who spoke to her: 'You are the God who sees me,' for she said, 'I have now seen the One who sees me.'"—Genesis 16:13 (NIV)

Devotional Reflection:

There's a silence that doesn't bring peace, a silence that's born from fear, shame, or exhaustion. Maybe you've lived in that silence, afraid to speak up, unsure if your voice matters, or too worn down to explain your pain one more time. Maybe you got so used to being quiet that you forgot you had something worth saying.

But God sees what others overlook. He hears what's never said out loud. He listens to the sighs you release into your pillow, the tears that never make it to words, the ache you try to carry with dignity.

Hagar, the servant of Sarai, found herself running alone, pregnant, and invisible to those who should have protected her. She was used, dismissed, and cast aside. But in the wilderness, God found her. He didn't shame her. He didn't ignore her story. He called her by name and gave her a promise. In response, Hagar called Him *El Roi*, the God who sees me.

What a beautiful truth: the wilderness doesn't erase your worth; it reveals God's awareness.

You may feel forgotten, but God sees you. You may have silenced yourself to survive, but God invites you to speak again. Not for applause. Not for validation. But for healing. Your voice is not a liability. It's a lifeline. It carries the sound of your freedom.

There's something powerful about breaking the silence, not just with others, but within yourself. Naming your fears. Admitting your longings. Speaking your truth before God and trusting that He won't reject you for it. Some of the most powerful breakthroughs begin with a whisper: "God, I don't know what to say, but I'm tired of holding it all in."

This solo journey isn't about pretending to be okay. It's about finding the safety to say, "I'm not okay… but I'm healing." And healing starts when you're no longer afraid of your truth.

You've spent enough time shrinking. Enough time minimizing your pain to make others comfortable. Enough time hiding behind strength that's just been survival in disguise.

God isn't afraid of your honesty. He meets you at the well like He met Hagar, offering hope in place of shame, clarity in place of confusion, identity in place of invisibility.

Let today be the day you speak again over yourself, over your future, over the wounds you thought you had to keep quiet. Declare your healing out loud. Name your worth again. Speak life where silence used to live. Because your voice is sacred. And it's time to let it rise.

Journal Prompts:

1. What silence have you been carrying?

____

____

____

____

____

____

2. If you could say anything without fear of judgment, what would you say?

____

____

____

____

____

____

3. Where in your life do you need to be reminded that God sees you?

____

____

____

____

____

____

Prayer:

El Roi, the God who sees me, thank You for seeing what others missed. For hearing the cries, I never said out loud. I've spent so long hiding my voice, afraid it wasn't worth hearing. But today, I choose to believe You are calling me to speak again.

Not for validation, but for healing. I release the fear, the shame, and the silence I've carried for too long. Give me the courage to speak my truth to You, to myself, and to the places that need freedom. Meet me in the wilderness like You met Hagar. Show me that my voice matters, and my story still holds purpose. In Jesus' name, Amen.

Journal Notes:

Journal Notes:

Day 62:

Becoming Bold

Scripture:

"The righteous are as bold as a lion."—Proverbs 28:1b (NIV)

Devotional Reflection:

There is a boldness being birthed in you, not arrogance, not performance, but holy courage. The kind that comes when you've been quiet too long, when you've questioned your worth, and when you've decided to finally reclaim it.

It's the kind of boldness that's rooted in identity, not insecurity. It doesn't seek the spotlight; it answers a divine call. It doesn't need a crowd to confirm it, just the whisper of God's voice reminding you: *You were made for this.*

Boldness doesn't mean you have all the answers. It means you show up anyway. It means you walk into rooms you once thought were too big for you and take your seat without apology. It means you stop waiting to be chosen and start living like you already are.

Think of Esther, an orphan, taken into the palace, hesitant at first to risk her position or her life. She could've stayed silent. She could've stayed safe. But when Mordecai reminded her of her purpose, something shifted. She rose up, stepped out, and spoke up, not because she wasn't afraid, but because her calling was louder than her fear.

Esther's story reminds us that boldness is born in the tension between comfort and calling. And this solo journey is calling you to rise in the same way. To stop tiptoeing around your destiny. To stop editing yourself to make others more comfortable. To step into your own "for such a time as this" moment without shrinking. Without explaining. Without guilt.

God didn't create you to play small. He created you to carry light. To carry truth. To carry impact. And the world needs what's inside you, even the parts still in progress.

Boldness isn't always loud. Sometimes it's quiet and steady, setting boundaries, saying no, or simply showing up as your true self. It looks like refusing to apologize for your presence. It looks like honoring your voice, even when it shakes. It looks like choosing obedience over fear, and truth over silence.

You are allowed to be bold. Not just for others but for yourself. You are allowed to take up space. To speak with authority. To walk in confidence. Because you are not just a woman finding her way, you are a woman becoming who God designed you to be.

And when the fear rises and it will, remember that you're not walking alone. God goes before you. His Spirit lives within you. His strength is made perfect in every shaky step you take.

So, rise up, woman of purpose. This world needs your voice. And your boldness is not just about today; it's a legacy you're building for generations to come.

Journal Prompts:

1. What is one area of your life where you've been shrinking back?

   ____
   ____
   ____
   ____
   ____
   ____

2. What would boldness look like for you this week?

   ____
   ____
   ____
   ____
   ____
   ____

3. How can you remind yourself that God has already equipped you?

   ____
   ____
   ____
   ____
   ____
   ____

Prayer:

God, give me holy boldness, the kind that isn't rooted in ego, but in purpose. Help me walk into rooms with confidence, not because I'm perfect, but because I'm called. Just like Esther, let me rise to the occasion and speak with courage, knowing

You are with me. I release fear and step into the fullness of who You created me to be. Let my boldness glorify You and inspire others to do the same. In Jesus' name, Amen.

Journal Notes:

Journal Notes:

Day 63:

Layers of Healing

Scripture:

"But I will restore you to health and heal your wounds, 'declares the Lord,"—Jeremiah 30:17a (NIV)

Devotional Reflection:

Healing isn't always linear. It happens in layers, like peeling back the petals of a flower or unwrapping the chapters of a long and complex story. Just when you think you've arrived, a new layer is revealed. Not because you're failing but because God is going deeper. Because there is more freedom for you to discover.

Maybe you've asked, "Why am I still feeling this?" or "I thought I was over that." You might feel frustrated when old wounds reopen or when unexpected triggers surface. But healing isn't a one-time event. It's a sacred unfolding, a holy unraveling of what was buried, so God can restore what was broken.

Each layer is an invitation. An invitation to trust God in new places. To feel instead of numb. To rest instead of strive. To allow the deeper parts of your soul to come into the light and be loved, not judged.

Think of Mary Magdalene, a woman once tormented, overlooked, and bound by darkness. Jesus delivered her from seven demons, and her transformation didn't just stop at deliverance, it grew into devotion. She stayed close to Him. She listened. She wept. She followed all the way to the tomb. And because of her unwavering love and loyalty, she became the first to witness the resurrection.

Her story didn't end with being healed. It was just the beginning.

Your healing, too, has layers and each one brings you closer to wholeness, not farther from it. Just because it still hurts doesn't mean you're broken beyond repair. It means God is still working. Still cleansing. Still reshaping your heart.

Don't despise the parts that still sting. Don't rush to hide them. Bring them to Jesus. He knows what to do with wounds that feel too raw to explain. He doesn't roll His eyes at your triggers. He doesn't get tired of your tears. He sits with you in the middle of the mess and ministers to the pain no one else sees.

He doesn't rush the process because love is patient. And His love is perfect.

Sometimes healing looks like weeping over the same thing more than once. Sometimes it's realizing that even though you forgave, you still need to grieve. Sometimes it's celebrating your progress while still being honest about your pain.

God is not overwhelmed by the process. So, you don't need to be ashamed of it.

Your brokenness does not disqualify you. It's the very place where His love will meet you again and again. Every layer is an opportunity to discover how wide and deep His grace really goes.

You are not broken beyond repair. You are healing in His hands.

Journal Prompts:

1. What layers of pain or healing are resurfacing right now?

   ____
   ____
   ____
   ____
   ____
   ____

2. How have you seen growth in yourself, even in small ways?

   ____
   ____
   ____
   ____
   ____
   ____

3. What would it look like to be patient with your own process?

   ____
   ____
   ____
   ____
   ____
   ____

Prayer:

God, thank You for not giving up on my healing. Thank You for staying with me through every layer, through every tear, memory, and ache. I admit that sometimes I grow weary. I want to move on. I want to feel whole already. But You know what I need, and You love me enough to take Your time. Help me to trust the process, to be gentle with myself, and to believe that healing is still happening, even when it feels slow. Let every layer draw me closer to You and remind me that I am never beyond the reach of Your grace. In Jesus' name, Amen.

Journal Notes:

Journal Notes:

Day 64:

When You Feel Forgotten

Scripture:

"Can a mother forget the baby at her breast and have no compassion on the child she has borne? Though she may forget, I will not forget you!"—Isaiah 49:15 (NIV)

Devotional Reflection:

Being forgotten is one of the deepest wounds a heart can carry. It's not always about being left behind, it's about feeling unseen, uncared for, or overlooked in the moments that mattered most.

Maybe you've watched others move on while you were still stuck in the aftermath. Maybe people stopped checking in after the crisis passed. Maybe your name disappeared from their lists, their minds, their prayers. Maybe it wasn't loud, but the silence spoke volumes.

You've carried burdens in secret. You've loved quietly. You've shown up for people who didn't stay for you. You've poured out your strength and wondered if anyone noticed how empty you felt after.

But God hasn't forgotten. Not you. Not the prayers you whispered through tears. Not the sacrifices you made quietly behind the scenes. Not the parts of your heart you gave without ever asking for anything in return.

He remembers every silent ache. Every overlooked effort. Every tear you thought no one saw.
Everyone seems to forget fast, God remembers well. He doesn't just think of you occasionally, He has engraved your name on the palms of His hands. That means you're not just remembered, you're carried.

Think about that: You are literally written into the hands of God. What could be more intimate? What could be more permanent?

Remember Hannah? She was a woman of deep longing. Year after year, she returned to the temple with the same broken prayer for a child. She was mocked, misunderstood, even accused of being drunk in her grief. But Scripture says, *"The Lord remembered her."*

He didn't just remember the words she said, He remembered her whole heart. And in the right time, her waiting turned into a promise fulfilled.

God sees you the same way. Even in the places where nothing seems to be happening, He is working behind the scenes. Even when the silence feels loud and lonely, heaven is not ignoring you.

You are not forgotten. You are held. Seen. Known. Cherished.

So don't measure your worth by who checks in. Don't base your value on who shows up for you or how long you've been waiting. Anchor your identity in the unwavering truth that God never looks away.

Even when others move on, God stays. Even when they forget, He remembers.

And sometimes the delay is not a denial, it's a setup for something greater. You're not behind. You're being prepared. You're not overlooked, you're being positioned.

You are not forgotten. You are beloved.

Journal Prompts:

1. Where in your life have you felt forgotten or overlooked?

____

____

____

____

____

____

2. How does it comfort you to know that God remembers even the smallest details about you?

____

____

____

____

____

____

3. What prayer or promise are you holding onto, even in the silence?

____

____

____

____

____

____

Prayer:

Father, thank You for being the God who never forgets. When others move on, You remain. When I feel unseen, You see me fully. Remind me that I am not abandoned or overlooked. Write this truth on my heart: I am engraved on Your hands. Teach me to trust that You are working, even when it feels like nothing is moving. Help me find peace in Your presence and hope in Your remembrance. In Jesus' name, Amen.

Journal Notes:

____
____
____
____
____
____
____
____
____
____
____
____
____
____
____
____
____
____

Journal Notes:

Day 65:

Obedience in Motion

Scripture:

"The steps of a good man are ordered by the Lord, and He delights in his way."
—Psalm 37:23 (NKJV)

Devotional Reflection:

Sometimes the journey feels overwhelming, not because you lack the desire to grow, but because you don't know where to begin. You stand at the edge of change, and it all looks too big. Too far. Too uncertain.

Maybe you've whispered, "Where do I even start?"
Maybe your heart is willing, but your courage feels thin.
Maybe you've stared down the road ahead and felt paralyzed by all the unknowns.

But here's the truth: God never asked you to leap the entire mountain. He's not demanding perfection or performance. He's simply inviting you to take *one step*.

Just one.
The step that feels small but keeps you moving.
The step that seems quiet but carries spiritual weight.

One step in faith is enough to shift the atmosphere. Heaven responds when you move in obedience, no matter how timid that movement may feel.

Ruth understood this. She had every reason to stay where she was, grief, loss, and uncertainty surrounded her. But she took one courageous step away from the familiar and towards something she could not yet see. She didn't have a map. She didn't have a guarantee. All she had was a whisper in her spirit that staying where she was would no longer serve where God was leading.

Her "yes" was not loud. It wasn't flashy. But it was faithful. And that one step following Naomi to Bethlehem became the step that changed everything.

She didn't just walk into a new land. She walked into divine alignment.
She didn't just move forward; she moved into the lineage of Jesus.

What about you?
What if the breakthrough you've been praying for is waiting on the other side of your *next step*?

Maybe it's making the phone call.
Maybe it's enrolling in that class.
Maybe it's deleting the number.
Maybe it's trying again.
Maybe it's resting.
Maybe it's surrendering.
Maybe it's speaking the truth, even with a shaking voice.

Don't wait until you have the whole blueprint.
Don't talk yourself out of progress because the path ahead is unclear.
The light will meet you as you move.

Remember, God orders your steps, not your leaps, not your sprints.
Just your *steps*.

So, take one.
Take the one in front of you.
The one that's been nudging your spirit.
The one that's been showing up in your prayers.

There is breakthrough in the next step.
Not the perfect step.
Not the dramatic step.
Just the obedient one.

God doesn't require your certainty, only your surrender.
He will meet you in your movement.
And where He leads, grace will always follow.

Journal Prompts:

1. What step has God been gently nudging you to take, but fear or uncertainty has delayed?

   ____
   ____
   ____
   ____
   ____
   ____

2. What "Ruth moment" have you faced in your life, a time when you had to leave something behind and move forward in faith?

   ____
   ____
   ____
   ____
   ____
   ____

3. What would it look like to take one simple, obedient step this week toward your healing, growth, or purpose?

____

____

____

____

____

____

Prayer:

Father, thank You for ordering my steps, even when I feel unsure or afraid. I confess that sometimes I wait for clarity before I move, but today, I choose to trust You in the mystery. Help me to take the next step, no matter how small it seems. Remind me that obedience is more powerful than certainty, and that You meet me in motion. Give me the strength to move forward with faith, trusting that You are already on the other side of my step. In Jesus' name, Amen.

Journal Notes:

____

____

____

____

____

____

____

____

Journal Notes:

Day 66:

The Gift of Safe Community

Scripture:

"Two are better than one… If either of them falls down, one can help the other up." —Ecclesiastes 4:9–10 (NIV)

Devotional Reflection:

A solo journey doesn't mean isolation; it means intentionality. Even Jesus, who slipped away to solitary places for prayer, always returned to share meals, miracles, and heavy moments with trusted friends. Healing thrives in safe community spaces where vulnerability is met with honor and accountability is wrapped in compassion.

For years you may have worn masks just to survive, fearing judgment if the real story surfaced. Safe community dismantles that fear. It is the circle that cradles your story, prays when your words run out, and speaks truth when the lies get loud. In such company, shame loses its grip and courage multiplies.

Yet safe circles rarely appear magically; they're cultivated. You plant seeds of authenticity, water them with consistency, and protect them with boundaries. God often sends allies disguised as ordinary people: a mentor, a small-group sister, or a coworker turned confidante. Trust is built one honest conversation at a time.

Community is not weakness; it's wisdom in action. Even strong women need shoulders to lean on. Even bold voices need soft places to rest. We were designed for interdependence. The lone-wolf myth sounds heroic, but in reality, it keeps wounds hidden and hearts malnourished.

Safe community is reciprocal. You're called not only to be supported but also to be a support. As iron sharpens iron, God places you in relationships where mutual edification is the goal. You become an encourager, a listener, a lifter. Healing becomes contagious. When one soul heals, another is inspired to do the same.

Of course, community is imperfect because people are imperfect. Misunderstandings happen; personalities clash. But when Christ is the center, humility, forgiveness, and unity prevail. The risk of connection is real, yet the reward being fully seen and fully loved, is worth it.

So, pursue the circle that calls you higher. Initiate coffee dates, join the Bible study, open your home, ask the hard question, and share the real answer. Cultivate the soil where authentic fellowship can flourish. Your future self and those you'll impact will thank you.

Journal Prompts:

1. Who currently embodies "safe community" in your life, and how can you invest in that relationship this week?

   ____
   ____
   ____
   ____

2. What fears or past hurts make vulnerability difficult for you? Bring them honestly to God.

3. List one practical step to either deepen an existing faith circle or seek a new one (e.g., join a small group, start a prayer trio, attend a ministry gathering).

Prayer:

Father, thank You for designing me for connection. Heal any wounds that make me hide and grant me discernment to recognize safe spaces. Lead me to relationships where authenticity is celebrated and growth encouraged. Teach me to give and receive support with grace, so together we mirror Your love to a world in need. In Jesus' name, Amen.

Journal Notes:

Day 67:

The Gift of Hidden Seasons

Scripture:
"He made everything beautiful in its time."—Ecclesiastes 3:11 (ESV)

Devotional Reflection:

Hidden seasons are hard. You're doing the work, but no one sees. You're praying, growing, becoming, but it feels like nothing is happening. No applause. No fruit. No affirmation. Just silence and stillness. And that silence can make you question everything, your calling, your value, even your progress.

But hidden doesn't mean forgotten.
Obscurity doesn't mean abandonment.
Silence is not always rejection, it's often *refinement.*

God does some of His deepest, most powerful work in quiet places.
Before David ever wore a crown, he was in the fields learning how to worship, how to fight lions, how to be faithful in the unseen.
Before Joseph interpreted dreams in the palace, he endured betrayal, slavery, and isolation, all while keeping his integrity intact.
Before Jesus ever performed a miracle or preached to the

masses, He spent 30 years in quiet obedience growing in wisdom and stature, waiting for the appointed time.

The world celebrates the visible. God builds in the invisible.

Don't despise your hidden season; it's *preparation*, not punishment.
This is where roots grow deep.
Where ego dies and character is formed.
Where your identity is no longer anchored in applause, but in *who God says you are.*

There's something sacred about the seasons where it's just you and God. No spotlight. No noise. No likes or shares. Just process. Just presence.
It may not be glamorous, but it's *holy.*

You are not being overlooked. You are being *refined.*
You are not behind schedule; you are *on heaven's timeline.*
And what feels like delay may actually be divine development, God crafting something that cannot be rushed.

The bamboo plant stays underground for years before it ever shoots up. But when it finally breaks through the soil, it grows rapidly because its root system had time to strengthen.

So, stay rooted. Stay faithful.
Don't rush out of what God is using to *build* you.
He is not just preparing the promise for you; He's preparing *you* for the promise.

When the time is right, what's been planted in secret will bloom in public.
And when it does, it will be evident that the wait wasn't a waste, it was *wisdom.*

Trust the timing.
Trust the process.
Trust the *Gardener.*

Journal Prompts:

1. How have you viewed hidden seasons in your life, frustrating or formative?

   ____
   ____
   ____
   ____
   ____
   ____

2. What has God taught you in seasons where no one else seemed to notice your growth?

   ____
   ____
   ____
   ____
   ____
   ____

3. In what ways are you being prepared now for what you've prayed for later?

   ____
   ____
   ____
   ____
   ____
   ____

Prayer:

God, remind me that the hidden places are not empty, they're holy. Help me not to rush past what You're developing in me just because it feels quiet. Teach me to trust that Your timing is always right and that the silence doesn't mean You've stopped working. Grow me. Ground me. Refine me. And when the time is right, let what You've cultivated in secret bring You glory. In Jesus' name, Amen.

Journal Notes:

Journal Notes:

Day 68:

You're Allowed to Change

Scripture:

"Therefore, if anyone is in Christ, the new creation has come: The old has gone, the new is here!"—2 Corinthians 5:17 (NIV)

Devotional Reflection:

You're allowed to change.
You're allowed to grow.
You're allowed to outgrow the places, habits, and even relationships that no longer align with the woman God is forming you into.
Change isn't betrayal; it's becoming.

Spiritual maturity will require you to shift. And while the world might resist your evolution, heaven rejoices over it. God never intended for you to remain stagnant, stuck, or squeezed into the mold of who you were. Growth is not rebellion; it's revelation. It's the unveiling of who you *really* are in Him.

There will be people who try to hold you hostage to your past, people who only know the old version of you and aren't willing to meet the new one. They'll say things like, "You've changed," with suspicion or disappointment, as if staying the same is somehow the goal. But don't let that shame you. That's not a rebuke; it's confirmation.

Transformation is the evidence that God is at work.
You were never meant to stay the same.
You were *designed* to evolve.

The process of sanctification is not instant; it's continual. You may not notice it overnight, but little by little, God is shaping your thoughts, healing your wounds, softening your heart, and enlarging your spirit. And as that happens, your tastes will change. Your boundaries will shift. Your discernment will sharpen. What once felt comfortable may now feel constraining, and that's okay. It doesn't mean something is wrong. It means something is working.

Lot's wife looked back and turned to salt, not because her body turned, but because her *heart* did. She longed for what was behind her, even though God had called her forward. The same can happen to us when we cling to expired seasons, familiar dysfunctions, or outdated versions of ourselves. At some point, you have to let go, not because you're heartless, but because you're *healing*.

Release the pressure to explain your growth to people who aren't growing.
Release the guilt that whispers you're "too much" now.
Release the fear that your next level will leave others behind.

You don't need permission to evolve.
You don't need a committee to confirm your calling.
You just need the courage to say yes when God says, "It's time."

This journey is not about becoming who others expect you to be; it's about becoming who God *created* you to be.
So keep going.
Even if your voice shakes.
Even if the path is unfamiliar.
Even if you walk alone.

You're not being fake.
You're becoming *free.*
And your freedom is not just for you; it's a light for someone else still stuck in their past.

Journal Prompts:

1. In what ways have you grown that you're afraid others won't understand or accept?

   ____
   ____
   ____
   ____
   ____
   ____

2. Are there old versions of yourself you're still clinging to out of fear or guilt?

   ____
   ____
   ____
   ____
   ____
   ____

3. What would it look like to fully embrace the woman you're becoming in Christ?

   ____
   ____
   ____
   ____
   ____
   ____

Prayer:

Father, thank You for the freedom to grow. I release the fear of judgment and the pressure to stay the same for the comfort of others. Help me to embrace the woman You are shaping me into. Give me the courage to let go of what no longer aligns with my purpose. I choose transformation. I choose truth. I choose You. In Jesus' name, Amen.

Journal Notes:

Journal Notes:

Day 69:

When the Wait Feels Too Long

Scripture:

"Let us not become weary in doing good, for at the proper time we will reap a harvest if we do not give up."
—Galatians 6:9 (NIV)

Devotional Reflection:

Waiting is one of the hardest parts of the journey.

It tests your hope.
It stretches your faith.
It reveals your trust.
It presses on every part of you that wants control, certainty, and immediacy.

Waiting doesn't just challenge your patience; it challenges your perspective. You start to wonder: *Did I hear God right? Did I miss my moment? Is something wrong with me?*
You've prayed with tears in your eyes.
Sowed seeds with trembling hands.
Held onto promises when everything in you screamed to let go.
And still, heaven seems silent.
Still, the answer hasn't arrived.
Still, the door remains closed.

But hear this clearly: Silence is not absence.
And delay is not denial.

God's "not yet" is not a punishment, it's preparation.
He's not punishing you by making you wait, He's perfecting something in you.

In this in-between space where nothing feels certain and you're tempted to quit; God is working behind the scenes in ways you cannot see.
He's aligning circumstances.
He's developing your character.
He's stretching your capacity so you can hold the very thing you've been praying for.

Waiting is holy ground.
It is sacred soil where trust is deepened, and faith is proven.
It's where you choose to worship even when you don't understand.
Where you cling to hope even when nothing seems to be happening.

Look at Sarah, she laughed at the idea of giving birth in her old age, and yet *God did it anyway*. Her laughter of doubt became a laughter of joy.
Joseph endured betrayal, slavery, and years in prison, but he didn't stop serving faithfully and *God promoted him anyway*.
Even Jesus, the Son of God waited three decades before stepping into His public purpose. Waiting was not beneath Him, and it is not beneath us.

What if this season isn't about what's missing, but about what's being made?
What if the breakthrough isn't being delayed; it's being custom designed for your future?

Don't mistake God's process for His absence.
Don't give up because you don't see the fruit yet.
You're still in the soil season and things grow slow in the soil.

The harvest is still coming.
Keep watering it with prayer.
Keep guarding it with faith.
Keep protecting it with obedience.

Don't walk away from the field before the fruit appears.

Journal Prompts:

1. What are you waiting on God for in this season?

   ____
   ____
   ____
   ____
   ____
   ____

2. How has the waiting stretched or strengthened your faith?

   ____
   ____
   ____
   ____
   ____
   ____

3. In what ways can you remain obedient and faithful while you wait?

   ____
   ____
   ____
   ____
   ____
   ____

Prayer:

God, waiting is hard. It stirs up my fears, my doubts, and my impatience. But today, I choose to trust that You are still working, even when I can't see it. Help me not to confuse silence with absence or delay with denial. Teach me to lean into Your process and believe that You are preparing something greater than I could imagine. Strengthen me to wait well with faith, with hope, and with obedience. I trust that what You've promised will come to pass in Your perfect time. In Jesus' name, Amen.

Journal Notes:

Journal Notes:

Day 70:

You're Stronger Than You Think

Scripture:

"The Lord gives strength to his people; the Lord blesses his people with peace." — Psalm 29:11 (NIV)

Devotional Reflection:

You may not feel strong right now.
You might feel tired, discouraged, worn thin by life.
Like you're just barely making it through the day; emotionally drained, spiritually weary, and unsure how much longer you can hold it together.

But strength isn't always loud.
It's not always found in big victories or bold declarations.
Sometimes it looks like holding back tears in the middle of a meeting.
Sometimes it's choosing to hope when everything feels hopeless.
Sometimes it's whispering a prayer through clenched teeth and tear-stained cheeks.

Strength is the quiet defiance of faith in the face of darkness.
It's refusing to quit even when quitting would be easier.

It’s the courage to rise again, not because you feel ready, but because you trust the One who strengthens you.

You may feel like you’re falling apart, but God sees a woman who’s still fighting.
Still showing up.
Still choosing to believe.
And *that* is strength.

The enemy loves to whisper lies when you're weary.
He’ll tell you you’re not enough.
That you’ll never get back what you lost.
That the pain will last forever.
But he underestimates the God who lives within you.

You carry resurrection power.
You house the Spirit of the Living God.
You are not fragile, you are *Spirit-fortified.*

You’re not operating on your own limited strength; you’re anchored to a limitless Source.

When Paul said, “*I will boast all the more gladly about my weaknesses, so that Christ’s power may rest on me,*” (2 Corinthians 12:9) he wasn’t celebrating struggle, he was celebrating supernatural strength that shows up in human limitations.

What if this season of weakness is your setup for divine strength?
What if your breaking is making room for breakthrough?

You don’t have to fake strength.
You just have to stay connected to the One who *is* strong.

Your strength doesn't come from striving; it comes from surrender.
Let go of what's too heavy.
Lay down what was never yours to carry.
Lean into the grace that doesn't run out.
God's strength is made perfect right here in the middle of your mess.

So, breathe. Cry if you need to. Rest if you must.

But don't forget this:

You are stronger than you think because God is stronger than you know.

And He lives in you.

Journal Prompts:

1. In what ways have I been underestimating my own strength in this season?

   ____
   ____
   ____
   ____
   ____
   ____

2. Where have I been striving instead of surrendering?

   ____
   ____
   ____
   ____
   ____

3. How can I practically lean into God's strength instead of my own today?

Prayer:

Father, I admit that I feel weak. Tired. Stretched. But thank You that my weakness is not a liability, it's a place where Your power can rest. Help me stop striving to be strong in my own ability and instead surrender to Your supernatural strength. Remind me that even on my lowest days, You are lifting me, holding me, carrying me. Let Your grace be my anchor and Your power my portion. I don't want to just survive, I want to trust You fully in the storm. Make me strong in You, Lord. In Jesus' name, Amen.

Journal Notes:

Journal Notes:

Day 71:

This Is Part of the Plan

Scripture:

"And we know that in all things God works for the good of those who love him, who have been called according to his purpose."—Romans 8:28 (NIV)

Devotional Reflection:

You didn't expect this chapter.
Not the silence.
Not the tears you cry in the dark.
Not the doors that didn't open.
Not the people who walked away.
Not the dream that feels like it's drifting further out of reach.

You planned, prayed, and prepared, but *this* is not what you pictured.
Maybe this chapter feels unfamiliar, unfair, or even unbearable.
But hear this: just because it's not what you expected doesn't mean it's not what God ordained.

This is not a mistake.
It's not a detour.
It's a *divine setup.*

God is still God in this unexpected stretch.
He's not just the Author of the breakthroughs, He's the Author of the in-between, the not-yets, and the "what is this?" seasons too.

Think of Joseph.
He didn't ask for betrayal.
He didn't anticipate the pit.
He didn't deserve the prison.
But all along, God was doing what Joseph couldn't see, *positioning him for the palace.*

What looked like misfortune was really momentum.
What seemed like rejection was actually redirection.
And the same is true for you.

This isn't a breakdown, it's a build-up.
This season is preparing you to carry what you prayed for with *strength*, *wisdom*, and *humility*.
You're not just being delayed, you're being *developed.*

God doesn't just work in the spotlight; He works in the shadows.
He shapes character in the quiet.
He teaches trust in the tension.
He anchors faith in the fog.

So, if you're asking, *"God, how did I end up here?"*
Know that "here" is not your final destination.
"Here" is holy ground.
"Here" is where He's strengthening your roots.
"Here" is where He's making you ready.

Even when it feels slow, God is not stalled.
Even when you feel overlooked, God has His eyes on you.

Even when your heart aches, God is still good.
And yes, even now, you are still in His hands.

Journal Prompts:

1. In what ways does this current chapter feel disappointing or confusing? Write out your honest thoughts to God.

____
____
____
____
____
____

2. Can you look back and see a time when something unexpected actually turned out to be necessary?

____
____
____
____
____
____

3. What might God be developing in you during this "solo" stretch?

____
____
____
____
____
____

Prayer:

God, I didn't see this season coming, but I trust that You did. Help me to release my grip on what I thought life would look like. Remind me that You are just as present in the pauses and pits as You are in the promises fulfilled. Give me faith to believe that even this chapter has purpose. That even the parts that feel broken are being held together by Your hand. Strengthen my heart when I feel weary. Quiet my soul when I feel lost. And help me remember, this isn't the end of the story. You are still writing, still redeeming, still working. I surrender this unexpected chapter to You. In Jesus' name, Amen.

Journal Notes:

Journal Notes:

Day 72:

The Mirror of Grace

Scripture:

"Those who look to him are radiant; their faces are never covered with shame."—Psalm 34:5 (NIV)

Devotional Reflection:

There are days when you look in the mirror and don't recognize who you see.
The cracks feel too deep.
The weight of what you've been through is written in your eyes.
You carry silent battles, invisible bruises, and memories that don't seem to fade.
You wonder, *"Who am I now?"*
"Will I ever feel whole again?"

But grace doesn't flinch at your reflection.
It doesn't pull away from your broken places.
It draws closer.
It whispers, *"You are still mine, even here. Especially here."*

Grace is not repelled by your wounds, it is drawn to them.
Where the world says, "Cover that up," grace says, "Let Me touch it."
Where shame says, "Hide," grace says, "Heal."

God is not intimidated by what's been broken in you.
He specializes in redemption.

The world teaches us to perform, to impress, to be polished and perfect.
But God is not looking for performance, He's looking for surrender.
He doesn't anoint the flawless; He anoints the *willing*.

Think of Rahab.
A woman with a past.
A label.
A reputation that could've disqualified her.
But God rewrote her story and wove her into His.
She wasn't just saved, she was *chosen*.
Not in spite of her past, but through it.

If God can turn Rahab's mess into a miracle,
If He can take a broken woman and make her part of the Messiah's lineage,
Then surely, He can do the same with you.

God sees your full story, every page, every mistake, every detour, and still calls you worthy.

Stop disqualifying yourself because of what you've been through.
Stop comparing your process to someone else's perfection.
Their highlight reel isn't proof of their worth, just as your hidden pain isn't proof of your lack.

Grace is your mirror now.
And when you look through the lens of grace, you'll see something the world can't explain:

A woman who is being shaped, not shamed.
Formed, not forgotten.
Held, not hidden.

You are not what happened to you.
You are not the names they called you.
You are not the things you lost.

You are the one God chose to redeem, restore, and rewrite.

So, look again.
Look past the cracks.
Look deeper than the pain.
And you'll see evidence that God is still working, still loving you through it all.

Journal Prompts:

1. Where have I allowed shame to become part of my identity?

   ____
   ____
   ____
   ____
   ____
   ____

2. What would change if I saw myself the way God sees me through the lens of grace?

   ____
   ____
   ____
   ____
   ____

3. How might God be using my brokenness as part of my calling?

Prayer:

Father, thank You for seeing me fully and still calling me worthy. On the days I can't recognize myself, help me to look through Your eyes of grace. Remind me that You are not repelled by my past or disappointed by my wounds. You are the God who restores what's broken and uses it for glory. Like Rahab, I give You my history and ask You to write purpose into every page. Help me silence the lies of shame and listen to the voice of truth. I am not forgotten. I am not finished. I am Yours. In Jesus' name, Amen.

Journal Notes:

Journal Notes:

Day 73:

Stop Shrinking

Scripture:

"You are the light of the world. A town built on a hill cannot be hidden."—Matthew 5:14 (NIV)

Devotional Reflection:

You weren't created to shrink.
You were never meant to blend in, back down, or be silent about the fire God placed inside you.
But somewhere along the way, you learned to dim your light, to make others comfortable, to avoid criticism, to protect yourself from disappointment or rejection.
You started thinking *"too much"* was a flaw, when in reality, *"too much"* was a mark of your divine design.

But shrinking doesn't serve the Kingdom.
It only stifles the gift.
And what God placed inside you was meant to multiply, not stay hidden under layers of fear or false humility.

Even Moses tried to hide.
"Who am I?" he asked, not out of reverence, but out of resistance.
He focused on his lack instead of God's sufficiency.

He doubted his voice when God had already declared His plan.

And don't we do the same?

We say:
"I'm not ready."
"I'm not enough."
"Someone else could do this better."

But God says:
"I chose you."
"I will go with you."
"I put My words in your mouth."

God isn't impressed by perfection; He's moved by obedience.
He's not waiting for you to have all the answers.
He's waiting for you to say *yes*, even with trembling hands and an unsure heart.

You may feel unworthy of the platform, the purpose, or the promise.
But hear this: You don't have to earn what God has already assigned.
The calling on your life isn't about your résumé, it's about your *readiness to surrender.*

God knew who you were before you ever failed, hesitated, or shrunk back.
And still, He called you.

So, it's time to stop apologizing for the way you shine.
It's not pride; it's *purpose.*
It's not arrogance; it's *anointing.*
Let your light reflect the One who lit it.

There are people who need what you carry.
There are souls attached to your "yes."
You were not created to play small in a Kingdom that's advancing.
You were created to move mountains, speak boldly, love fiercely, and lead freely.

So, walk in it.
Live like you believe it.
Own your light.
And never forget your brilliance brings Him glory.

Journal Prompts:

1. Where in my life have I been shrinking, silencing, or dimming my light to make others comfortable?

____
____
____
____
____
____

2. What have I been disqualifying myself from that God has already called me to?

____
____
____
____
____
____

3. How can I show up more boldly in the spaces where I've been playing small?

____

____

____

____

____

____

Prayer:

Father, forgive me for the times I've shrunk back from the calling You placed on my life. I've questioned my worth, silenced my voice, and allowed fear to shape my decisions. But I'm ready to walk differently now. Remind me that You don't call the perfect, you call the willing. Help me to stop dimming what You lit within me. Help me to step into rooms boldly, knowing I carry Your Spirit. Let my confidence be rooted not in my ability, but in Your authority. I want to shine, not for applause, but for Your glory. In Jesus' name, Amen.

Journal Notes:

____

____

____

____

____

____

____

____

Journal Notes:

Day 74:

The Pause That Heals

Scripture:

"Be still, and know that I am God..."—Psalm 46:10 (NIV)

Devotional Reflection:

When our communities praise multi-tasking, stillness feels like failure.
We're taught that movement means progress and that if we're not doing something visible, we must be falling behind. But on this solo journey, stillness is not a setback; it's sacred.

Stillness isn't empty.
Stillness is where Heaven meets your breath.

God doesn't always speak in the fire or the earthquake sometimes; it's the gentle whisper.
Elijah learned this in the cave.
Exhausted. Afraid. Alone.
He had just called down fire from heaven, and now he was hiding, weary from the weight of it all.
He wasn't met with a command to do more or go faster.
He was met with rest.
He was met with presence.

Sometimes, your next breakthrough won't come through striving, but through surrender.
You may be in a season where the silence feels loud. Where prayers feel unanswered, and the wait feels endless.
No new doors.
No clear direction.
No visible progress.

But stillness is not absence; it's *alignment*.
God is slowing you down to center you.
To ground you.
To remind you that your value isn't in what you *do* but in who you *are* in Him.

Stillness prepares the soil of your soul.
It reveals what busyness tried to bury.
It shows you what you've been running from and what God is trying to heal.
In stillness, your ears become uncluttered by the noise of comparison, and your heart becomes attuned to the rhythm of grace.

Think of Mary at Jesus' feet. While Martha was busy, distracted, and anxious, Mary chose stillness. And Jesus called it the *better part*.
Not because doing is bad, but because being with Him is the beginning of everything.

So don't run from this pause.
Don't rush to fill the silence.
Let the sacred slow do its work.

Let God restore the rhythm of your heart.
Let Him show you that waiting is not wasting; it's *weaving*.
He is threading wisdom, clarity, and strength into your spirit.

And when the time comes to move again, you'll rise not from depletion, but from *deep peace*.

Journal Prompts:

1. Where in my life do I feel the pressure to keep producing or performing?

   ____
   ____
   ____
   ____
   ____
   ____

2. What have I been avoiding in the silence that God may be trying to address?

   ____
   ____
   ____
   ____
   ____
   ____

3. What does stillness reveal about where I place my identity and worth?

   ____
   ____
   ____
   ____
   ____
   ____

Prayer:

God, I confess that stillness often makes me uncomfortable. I feel like I should be doing more, fixing more, achieving more. But today, I choose to rest in You. Quiet my anxious thoughts. Help me embrace this sacred pause, not as punishment but as preparation. Teach me to hear Your whisper again. Re-align my pace with Yours. Let this season of stillness become holy ground where I rediscover Your presence, Your peace, and my purpose. I trust You with the silence. I trust You with the slow. In Jesus' name, Amen.

Journal Notes:

Journal Notes:

Day 75:

You Are Not Too Much

Scripture:

"I praise you because I am fearfully and wonderfully made; your works are wonderful, I know that full well."
—Psalm 139:14 (NIV)

Devotional Reflection:

Have you ever been told you're "too much"?
Too emotional. Too passionate. Too intense. Too strong. Too bold. Too soft.
So you began to question:
Maybe I should tone it down...
Maybe I should take up less space...
Maybe being "less" will make me more lovable, more acceptable, more safe...

But what if your "too much" is actually just *right* for what God created you to do?

The enemy loves to label what he fears.
If he can convince you that your boldness is a burden, that your fire is a flaw, that your heart is a hindrance, then you'll spend your life hiding the very thing God placed in you to *heal the world.*

You are not too much. You are not a mistake. You are a masterpiece on purpose.

God didn't fumble when He made you passionate.
He didn't make a mistake when He gave you empathy.
He wasn't reckless when He gave you a voice that trembles with truth or a fire that refuses to go out.

He made you a storm because you were called to shift atmospheres.
You weren't made to fit into shallow boxes.
You were made to *overflow* with Spirit and purpose and power.

Think of the women God used:

- **Esther**—a woman with beauty *and* boldness. She risked her life to speak up, not because she was fearless, but because she was *called.*
- **Deborah**—a prophet and judge, who led men and women alike with strength, wisdom, and courage.
- **Mary**—a young woman who carried the Messiah in her womb, misunderstood and unseen by many, yet fully embraced by Heaven.

None of them were "too much."
They were *just enough* to carry the weight of their assignment.

So are you.

You are an answer to a problem God saw in the earth.
You are a vessel of justice, beauty, compassion, and power.
When your emotions are surrendered to the Spirit, they don't make you unstable, they make you *sensitive to what others*

ignore.
When your voice is yielded to God, it doesn't cause division, it brings *reformation*.
When your dreams are aligned with Heaven, they don't make you arrogant, they make you *dangerous to the kingdom of darkness*.

Stop apologizing for being who God created you to be.

You were never meant to dim.
You were meant to *disrupt*.
You were never meant to blend in.
You were meant to *build something bold*.
You were never meant to be manageable.
You were meant to be *moved by the Spirit*.

You are not "too much," you are *His masterpiece*. And that is more than enough.

Journal Prompts:

1. In what ways can your "too much" be a blessing to others when it's led by the Holy Spirit?

   ____
   ____
   ____
   ____
   ____
   ____

2. What would it look like for you to fully embrace and express the unique way God designed you without apology?

   ____

3. How can you begin to reclaim the parts of yourself you've hidden and use them boldly for God's Kingdom?

Prayer:

Father, forgive me for the times I shrunk myself to fit into rooms You never called me to stay in. For the times I hid my light, my voice, and my gifts just to make others comfortable. Help me see myself through Your eyes, not as "too much," but as *intentionally crafted*, *fearfully made*, and *fully loved*. Teach me to walk boldly in the fullness of who I am. To stop apologizing for the fire You've placed in me. To surrender my emotions, my voice, and my story for Your glory. Let me be a light that reflects You, unapologetic, unwavering, and unashamed. In Jesus' name, Amen.

Journal Notes:

Day 76:

You're Allowed to Be Both

Scripture:
"There is a time for everything, and a season for every activity under the heavens."—Ecclesiastes 3:1 (NIV)

Devotional Reflection:

On this journey, you may feel pressure to be either strong or soft.
To be either full of faith or weighed down by fear.
To smile through it all or crumble under the weight.
To have it all together or admit you're falling apart.
But here's the truth: you are allowed to be both.

You can be faithful and frustrated.
Grateful and grieving.
Hopeful and heartbroken.
Healing and still hurting.

This is the holy contradiction of being human and held by God.

We often think we have to pick a side, either/or.
But grace is not an ultimatum.
It's an invitation to show up as your *whole* self.

God never asked you to hide your wounds before entering His presence.
In fact, it's your *honesty* that invites His *healing*.

Look at Hannah.
She didn't filter her pain.
She didn't hide her tears.
She *poured* them out at the altar.
And in that sacred space of sorrow, God met her.
He didn't rebuke her anguish, He responded to it.

That's the kind of God you serve, One who doesn't ask you to choose between sorrow and strength.
He created you with the capacity for both.
For deep pain and deeper praise.
For weeping and still whispering *"I trust You."*

You are not weak for feeling.
You are not broken because you cry.
You are not less spiritual because you wrestle with doubt or fatigue or disappointment.

God is not looking for polished perfection.
He is moved by honest surrender.

Even Jesus, in the garden, felt the weight of agony and obedience.
He wept. He asked questions. He sweat blood.
And *He was still the Savior.*

So why do we believe we must be anything less than real?

You don't have to reduce to be accepted.
You don't have to pretend to be okay when you're not.
Your vulnerability is not a liability; it's a *bridge* to deeper intimacy with the Father.

You're not a contradiction.
You're a *testament*; a living, breathing story of grace holding tension.
And day by day, God is holding you together, even when it feels like you're falling apart.

Journal Prompts:

1. Where have you felt the pressure to "be okay" when you weren't?

   ____
   ____
   ____
   ____
   ____
   ____

2. In what ways are you both healing and still hurting and how can you offer that tension to God?

   ____
   ____
   ____
   ____
   ____
   ____

3. What would it look like to let grace hold your full truth today?

   ____
   ____
   ____
   ____
   ____
   ____

Prayer:

Father, thank You for meeting me right where I am, not where I pretend to be. I confess that sometimes I try to choose one side of the story to be either strong or struggling, either hopeful or hurting. But You remind me I don't have to choose. I can come to You in my complexity, and You won't turn me away. Teach me to rest in Your grace, to stop performing, and to simply be, fully known, fully loved, fully held. In the places where I feel torn, bring peace. In the places where I am weary, bring rest. In the places where I still ache, bring healing. Thank You for being a God who holds all of me, all at once. In Jesus' name, Amen.

Journal Notes:

Journal Notes:

Day 77:

Don't Rush the Becoming

Scripture:

"This vision is for a future time. It describes the end, and it will be fulfilled. If it seems slow in coming, wait patiently, for it will surely take place. It will not be delayed."
— Habakkuk 2:3 (NLT)

Devotional Reflection:

Growth takes time.

And let's be honest, it's not always easy to wait.

When most celebrate the quick win, the overnight success, the 30-day turnaround, we're taught that delay means defeat, that slowness means something's wrong.
But in God's kingdom, slow is not stuck.
It's sacred.

You may be praying, "God, why is this taking so long?"
And Heaven gently replies, "Because I'm building something that will *last.*"

You want to be healed already. Whole already. Living in the overflow already.
But friend, some breakthroughs are not microwaved, they're marinated.

You see, God doesn't just hand out victories.
He prepares you to *carry them.*

If you rush the process, you risk showing up unrooted, unready to sustain the very thing you asked Him for.
But when you submit to the *slow*, God does something deeper:
He strengthens your character.
He purifies your motives.
He trains your hands for the battle ahead.

Even Jesus waited.

The Son of God didn't start His public ministry until age 30.
He lived most of His life in obscurity, *becoming*, before He was revealed.
And when He finally stepped into the spotlight, He was grounded, focused, prepared.

The same is true for you.
Your quiet seasons are not wasted, they are wombs.
Where God forms identity.
Where He clarifies vision.
Where He breaks off what cannot go with you.

The world sees slow as failure.
But Heaven sees it as *formation.*

So don't despise the small steps.
The days that feel repetitive.
The progress that no one claps for.

Even a tree doesn't bear fruit every season, but it's still growing.
Roots deepening. Structure strengthening.

You are becoming, even in the dark.
You are becoming, even when no one notices.
You are becoming, even when it feels like nothing is changing.

God isn't impatient with your process.
He's committed to your transformation.

So, breathe. Be present. Let the slow work of grace do its perfect work in you.
You are not behind.
You are not forgotten.
You are not overlooked.

You're in the middle of something holy.
And it's worth the wait.

Journal Prompts:

1. Where do I feel rushed in my healing or growth journey?

 ____
 ____
 ____
 ____
 ____
 ____

2. What areas of my life do I need to surrender to God's perfect timing?

 ____
 ____
 ____
 ____

3. How can I begin to see my “slow seasons” as sacred and not shameful?

Prayer:

Lord, help me embrace the pace You’ve set for my life. Remind me that slow progress is still progress and that You are never in a hurry with what You’re healing and building in me. When I feel anxious, teach me to trust. When I feel behind, remind me that Your timing is always right. Let me find peace in the waiting, knowing You’re not just changing my circumstances, you’re transforming me. Thank You for being a God who is faithful to finish what You start. I am safe in Your process. In Jesus’ name, Amen.

Journal Notes:

Journal Notes:

Day 78:

Let the Walls Fall Down

Scripture:

"So do not fear, for I am with you; do not be dismayed, for I am your God. I will strengthen you and help you; I will uphold you with my righteous right hand."
—Isaiah 41:10 (NIV)

You built those walls for a reason.

Not out of weakness, but out of wisdom in the moment. You were doing what you had to do to keep going. To protect your heart from more damage. To shield your spirit from more disappointment. To survive the pain, you never saw coming.

And those walls did their job for a while. They gave you space to breathe, to function, to cope.

But now?

Those same walls are starting to feel like cages.
What once protected you is now isolating you.
The silence feels heavier. The numbness more constant.
And your heart, though hidden, is aching to be whole again.

Here's the truth: Healing requires access.
And God, so gentle, so patient refuses to force His way in.
He knocks. He waits.

Not because He lacks power, but because He desires partnership.
Your healing is holy ground, and He invites you to step onto it *with* Him.

Letting the walls down doesn't mean letting *everyone* in.
It means letting *God* in.
The One who sees every crack. Every brick. Every hidden wound behind it.
The One who isn't overwhelmed by your pain but deeply moved by it.

He's not asking for all of it today.
Just the first brick.
Just the first honest prayer.
Just the first step toward trust.

Remember Hannah?
She poured out her soul before the Lord, not polished, not composed.
But raw. Unfiltered. And *seen.*
That's where the healing began.

You don't have to hold it all together.
You don't have to present a version of yourself that's "fine."
You're allowed to bring your whole self, trembling, guarded, unsure.

Because the arms of God aren't just strong, they are *safe*.
Safe for your unraveling.
Safe for your doubt.
Safe for the places you've kept hidden for too long.

He doesn't discard the broken pieces, He rebuilds with them.
He doesn't minimize your trauma, He meets you in it.

And every wall you lower becomes a window for His presence to shine through.

This is your invitation.
Not to force healing but to *allow* it.
Not to rush the process but to *begin* it.

Brick by brick.
Tear by tear.
Surrender by surrender.

You don't have to be afraid of falling apart.
Because you're not falling into nothing, you're falling into grace.

Journal Prompts:

1. What is one "brick" I can lay down today to create more space for God's presence in my heart?

   ____

   ____

   ____

   ____

   ____

   ____

2. How have my walls kept out not only hurt, but also love and support?

   ____

   ____

   ____

   ____

   ____

   ____

3. In what ways has God already proven Himself to be a safe place for me, and how can I lean on that truth now?

____

____

____

____

____

____

Prayer:

Father, I've built these walls because I was trying to survive. I didn't know how else to protect myself. But now, they've become barriers between me and the healing I so deeply need. Today, I invite You in. Even if I can only open one small door, come in. I trust You to be gentle with my heart. Help me to feel safe in Your presence, to know that I don't have to hide or pretend with You. Begin Your healing work in me. Brick by brick, tear by tear, restore what's been broken. Make me whole again. In Jesus' name, Amen.

Journal Notes:

____

____

____

____

____

____

____

Journal Notes:

Day 79:

It's Safe to Hope Again

Scripture:

"Return to your fortress, you prisoners of hope; even now I announce that I will restore twice as much to you."
—Zechariah 9:12 (NIV)

Devotional Reflection:

When hope has disappointed you, it can feel easier to expect nothing.

You start to believe that numbness is safer than faith.
That detachment is wiser than vulnerability.
You tell yourself, *"If I stop hoping, I'll stop hurting."*

You've tasted the sting of unmet expectations.
You've cried prayers that felt like they bounced off the ceiling.
You've held onto promises that seem to be slipping through your fingers.
And so, bit by bit, you let your hope go quiet. You stop dreaming. You stop believing. You stop asking.

But *God never asked you to hope in outcomes.*
He asked you to hope in Him.

In His character.
In His unchanging nature.
In His goodness that doesn't waver with your circumstances.

Hope isn't blind optimism.
It's courageous trust.
It's choosing to believe, even while you're still bleeding.
It's the kind of faith that trembles but still stands.
Not because everything is perfect, but because God is still present.

Think of Abraham hoping against hope when there was no natural reason left to believe.
Think of Hannah praying for a child, year after year, despite the silence.
Think of Mary believing the angel's word, even when it disrupted everything she knew.

Hope is not passive.
It's fierce. It's resilient.
It's *warfare* against despair.

And even when your hands feel empty, your hope is doing holy work.
It's anchoring your soul to something greater than your current season.

God sees those dreams you buried under disappointment.
He knows how hard it was to let them go.
And yet, He whispers, *"It's safe to hope again."*

Not because you're guaranteed the exact outcome you once longed for—
But because *He* is trustworthy with your heart.
Because *He* restores what's been broken in ways more

beautiful than you imagined.
Because *He* never wastes your waiting.

Hope doesn't make you weak, it makes you brave.
It says, "Even if I'm still waiting, I believe You're working."
It declares, "Even if the answer is different than I expected, I know You are still good."

Be a *prisoner of hope*, not trapped by disappointment, but bound by expectancy.
Hope ties you to heaven's reality.
Hope keeps your spirit alive in the valley.
Hope is the seed that grows in dry ground, watered by faith and God's faithfulness.

And when God restores, He never does it halfway.

Journal Prompts:

1. Where have I given up hope because of past disappointment?

   ____
   ____
   ____
   ____
   ____
   ____

2. What dreams have I buried that God may be asking me to revisit with Him?

   ____
   ____
   ____
   ____

3. What does it look like for me to hope *in God*, not just for a specific outcome?

Prayer:

God, I confess, I've grown weary of hoping. It feels like too many times my heart has been met with silence. But today, I bring my hope back to You. Not to the outcomes I've desired, but to *You*, the One who holds all things together. I trust that You are good, even when things don't look the way I wanted them to. Give me the courage to believe again. Heal the parts of me that are afraid to hope. Remind me that You see what I've buried, and You're not done writing my story. Anchor my soul in You. Let my hope be a quiet strength, a bold trust, a sacred act of surrender. In Jesus' name, Amen.

Journal Notes:

Journal Notes:

Day 80:

You're Not Waiting in Vain

Scripture:

"But those who wait on the Lord shall renew their strength..."—Isaiah 40:31 (NKJV)

Devotional Reflection:

Waiting can feel like wasting, especially in a culture that glorifies movement.

We live in a time that celebrates constant movement, urgency, and visible progress.
If you're not producing, you're falling behind.
If you're not moving, you're losing.
So when God calls you into a season of stillness, it can feel like you're doing something wrong.

You may ask,
"What am I even doing here?"
"Why does it feel like everything has paused for me while life keeps going for everyone else?"
"What if I missed it? What if I'm behind?"

But beloved, waiting on God is never wasted time.
It's not a punishment. It's a holy invitation.
To be *with* Him before you do *for* Him.

To be *formed* before you are *sent*.
To be *rooted* before you *rise*.

Just like a seed planted deep in the soil, your growth may not be visible to others or even to yourself.
But God is doing something powerful beneath the surface.
Roots are developing. Character is maturing. Faith is being forged.
The waiting isn't empty. It's full of purpose.

God doesn't just prepare the promise; He prepares *you* for the promise.

And sometimes, that preparation requires stillness.
It requires trust when there are no signs.
It requires you to keep showing up in prayer, in obedience, in worship, even when nothing around you seems to change.

The world may not applaud your patience.
But heaven honors it.

The enemy will try to convince you that waiting equals delay, disappointment, or denial.
But God says, *"They that wait upon the Lord shall renew their strength"* (Isaiah 40:31).
Not just "survive the wait" but be *renewed* in it.

In the waiting, you're not forgotten. You're being formed.

God is stretching your endurance, strengthening your discernment, and teaching you how to hear His voice more clearly.
He's slowing you down so you don't run ahead of the blessing.
He's pruning the things that can't go with you to the next level.

He's positioning you for what you prayed for because He loves you too much to send you unprepared.

So don't curse the waiting.
Bless it. Steward it.
Learn in it. Grow in it. Worship through it.

When the door opens, when the season shifts, you'll be ready. Not just with opportunity in front of you, but with God's strength *within* you.

Don't rush the season. Wait well. Trust deeply.
God does His best work in the unseen.

Journal Prompts:

1. In what areas of my life am I being called to wait right now?

   ____
   ____
   ____
   ____
   ____
   ____

2. What lies have I believed about waiting that need to be surrendered?

   ____
   ____
   ____
   ____
   ____
   ____

3. How can I embrace this season of stillness as sacred instead of frustrating?

____

____

____

____

____

____

Prayer:

Lord, I confess, it's hard to wait. I've been conditioned to move fast, to make things happen, to measure my value by productivity. But You call me to a deeper pace, one that listens, trusts, and rests in You. Help me to see this waiting not as a delay, but as divine preparation. Anchor my heart in the truth that You are working, even when I can't see it. Teach me to wait well with hope, with expectation, with surrendered faith. I believe that You are forming me for something greater, and I choose to trust the process. In Jesus' name, Amen.

Journal Notes:

____

____

____

____

____

____

____

Journal Notes:

Day 81:

Your Yes Still Matters

Scripture:

"If you are willing and obedient, you will eat the good things of the land."—Isaiah 1:19 (NIV)

Devotional Reflection:

It's easy to think your small yes doesn't matter.
That your obedience goes unnoticed.
That your faithfulness in secret isn't producing anything worth celebrating.

But in the Kingdom of God, no yes is ever wasted.

He sees the prayers whispered in private.
The decisions made in silence.
The tears you cried behind closed doors when you chose obedience over comfort, surrender over control, truth over convenience.

Your quiet surrender is building something in the unseen.
Something holy. Something eternal.
Something that may not be visible now, but in time, will reveal the fingerprint of God's hand on your life.

Noah didn't just build a boat; he built history with his yes.
Ruth wasn't just loyal to Naomi, her yes grafted her into a

royal bloodline.
Mary wasn't just an obedient young woman, her yes made her the mother of our Redeemer.

They weren't seeking platforms or recognition.
They were just willing.
And their yes changed everything.

Every time you choose to obey, even when it's uncomfortable, even when it's not celebrated, even when it costs you relationships, opportunities, or your own plans, you are partnering with heaven.
You're saying, *"Not my will, but Yours be done."*
And that kind of yes moves mountains in the Spirit.

Obedience doesn't always come with applause or promotion.
Sometimes it looks like steady consistency, showing up again when you feel unseen.
Sometimes it looks like walking away from what's "almost right" so you can walk toward what's truly God.
Sometimes it means saying no to temporary satisfaction so you can say yes to lasting impact.

And sometimes, your yes is the key that unlocks breakthrough—
Not just for *you*, but for your children, your community, your legacy.

You never know what's riding on your yes.
A future you can't see yet.
A purpose you haven't fully stepped into.
A blessing that will flow to those connected to your life.

God isn't just watching what you do.
He's honoring *why* you do it.

And every time you surrender to His leading, heaven takes notice.

Keep saying yes. Even when it's hard. Even when it's hidden.
Because God sees. God honors.
And God always moves on the other side of obedience.

Journal Prompts:

1. What area of my life is God asking for a deeper yes right now?

   ____
   ____
   ____
   ____
   ____
   ____

2. Have I been underestimating the power of my obedience?

   ____
   ____
   ____
   ____
   ____
   ____

3. How can I remind myself that unseen faithfulness still carries eternal value?

   ____
   ____
   ____
   ____

Prayer:

Father, thank You for reminding me that no act of obedience is too small for You to use. Forgive me for the times I've doubted the significance of my yes. Help me to trust that even when no one else sees it, You do. Even when nothing seems to be changing, You are moving. Strengthen me to keep saying yes to You, especially when it's hard, hidden, or costly. Let my obedience echo beyond my own life, unlocking purpose and breakthrough for others. I surrender again today. My yes is Yours. In Jesus' name, Amen.

Journal Notes:

Journal Notes:

Day 82:

When You Feel Empty

Scripture:

"I went away full, but the Lord has brought me back empty."—Ruth 1:21 (NIV)

Devotional Reflection:

Naomi's words are painfully honest.
"I went away full, but the Lord has brought me back empty." (Ruth 1:21)
She left Bethlehem with a husband, two sons, and a future filled with promise.
She returned with grief in her bones and bitterness on her tongue.
She renamed herself "Mara," meaning bitter, because she no longer recognized the woman she had become.

Have you ever been there?

Where life has stripped you of what you once held dear?
Where it feels like everything that gave you identity, security, or joy has been lost?
Where even your prayers echo back in silence and your heart feels hollow?
That kind of emptiness can feel unbearable.
It can make you question your faith, your purpose, and even God's goodness.

But here's the truth:
God doesn't shame us for our emptiness. He steps into it.
He's not intimidated by your honesty.
He doesn't withdraw when you're bitter, broken, or barely holding on.
In fact, He draws near.

What Naomi couldn't see, what we often can't see in our lowest moments, was that her return marked the beginning of redemption, not just the end of what was.

She came back grieving, but she didn't come back alone.
Ruth walked beside her, a symbol of loyalty, love, and God's quiet faithfulness.
And woven into Naomi's loss was the seed of a legacy she couldn't have imagined.

Through Ruth came Boaz.
Through Boaz came Obed.
Through Obed came Jesse.
Through Jesse came David.
And through David… came **Jesus**.

What Naomi called empty, God called the beginning.

So, if you're feeling empty right now, if something's been taken from you, if loss has hollowed out your heart, if life didn't turn out the way you hoped, hear this:
This is not the end of your story.
God specializes in filling what feels void.

He pours beauty into broken places.
He turns graves into gardens.
He takes bitter chapters and pens redemption across the pages.

You may not see it yet, but God is already working behind the scenes.
He is aligning provision, preparing people, orchestrating moments that will restore, rebuild, and redeem.
Not just back to what was, but forward into what only He can do.

Your emptiness is not evidence that God has left.
It's often the very space where He begins to move.

Journal Prompts:

1. In what area of my life do I feel empty right now?

 ____
 ____
 ____
 ____
 ____
 ____

2. How might God be inviting me to see this emptiness as a beginning, not an end?

 ____
 ____
 ____
 ____
 ____
 ____

3. What has He redeemed in my past that I can remember and hold onto as hope?

 ____
 ____
 ____

Prayer:

Father, thank You that You don't turn away from my pain. Thank You for meeting me in the moments where I feel most empty, most lost, and most unsure. Help me to remember that emptiness isn't the end, it's often where You begin. Just like Naomi, I may not see the redemption yet, but I choose to trust that it's unfolding. Fill every hollow space in my heart with Your presence and remind me that nothing is wasted in Your hands. I may feel empty today, but I believe You are writing a story that leads to joy. In Jesus' name, Amen.

Journal Notes:

Journal Notes:

Day 83:
You Are Worth the Work

Scripture:

"So we rebuilt the wall till all of it reached half its height, for the people worked with all their heart."
—Nehemiah 4:6 (NIV)

Devotional Reflection:

Healing takes work. Growth takes intentionality. Boundaries take courage.
And sometimes, the deepest work is the most personal, the kind no one else can see but God.

When Nehemiah led the rebuilding of Jerusalem's walls, the work wasn't glamorous.
There were enemies mocking them, threatening them, trying to get them to stop.
There were moments when the builders had to hold a sword in one hand and a tool in the other (Nehemiah 4:17) fighting and building at the same time.

Doesn't healing feel like that sometimes?

You're trying to move forward, but the weight of the past still pulls at your heart.
You're laying bricks of new habits and healthier thoughts, while still dodging old triggers and spiritual warfare.

You're trying to protect your peace while repairing your brokenness.

It's not easy, but it is holy.

This journey of becoming whole isn't about perfection. It's about persistence.
It's choosing to show up for yourself, day by day, even when the process feels hard, lonely, or unseen.
Because *you* are the temple God is rebuilding. You are His beloved project.
And while others might not see the progress, heaven does.

Nehemiah's enemies tried to distract him with lies, lure him into arguments, and wear him down with fear.
But Nehemiah responded with this powerful declaration:
"I am doing a great work, and I cannot come down." (Nehemiah 6:3)

Let that be your posture.
When doubt rises, *I cannot come down.*
When the enemy whispers shame, *I cannot come down.*
When distractions try to derail your healing, *I cannot come down.*

Because the work you're doing, healing your heart, renewing your mind, setting boundaries, confronting trauma, learning to love yourself through God's lens; it matters.
It's not selfish. It's sacred.
Your freedom is worth fighting for.
Your wholeness is worth protecting.
Your future is worth every tear, every prayer, every step forward.

Don't let delay make you believe the work isn't worth it.
Don't let fatigue make you forget why you started.
Don't let discouragement make you put down your tools.

Keep building. Keep becoming. Keep healing.

God is with you on the wall.
And what He starts, He will finish.

Journal Prompts:

1. What part of my healing journey has felt the hardest and why?

   ____
   ____
   ____
   ____
   ____
   ____

2. In what areas have I seen God strengthening me, even if the work has been slow?

   ____
   ____
   ____
   ____
   ____
   ____

3. What "distractions" or lies do I need to shut out so I can keep building?

   ____
   ____
   ____

Prayer:

Father, thank You for being the Master Builder of my life. You see the parts of me I'm trying to rebuild the broken places, the wounded spaces, the habits I'm unlearning. Give me the strength to keep going when I feel weary. Help me to remember that this work is sacred and that my healing is important to You. Silence the voice of the enemy and every distraction that tries to pull me away from what You're doing in me. Let my spirit echo Nehemiah's words: "I am doing a great work, and I cannot come down." I choose to keep building with You by my side. In Jesus' name, Amen.

Journal Notes:

Journal Notes:

Day 84:

When You Don't Feel Qualified

Scripture:

"But Lord," Gideon asked, "how can I save Israel? My clan is the weakest...and I am the least in my family."
—Judges 6:15 (NIV)

Devotional Reflection:

Gideon's story hits close to home for many of us.
God calls him a "mighty warrior," but Gideon can't see it.
He looks around and sees his small tribe, his flawed past, his limited strength, and wonders if God has the wrong person.

Sound familiar?

You've felt the nudge to lead, serve, start, speak, shift, but doubt whispers, *"Why you?"*
You remember your failures. Your insecurities rise like giants. You don't feel brave, strong, or capable.
But here's the thing: God isn't speaking to who you used to be. He's speaking to who you *really are*.

When God called Gideon, He addressed him not by his fear, but by his *identity*, mighty warrior.
Even while Gideon was hiding, God saw a fighter. A leader. A vessel of deliverance.

Because God doesn't just see your now, He sees your *next*.

On your solo journey, there will be times when you feel inadequate for what lies ahead.
Your resume won't match the role.
Your history won't reflect your destiny.
Your confidence won't match the courage the assignment requires.

But hear this: God doesn't choose based on human standards.
He chooses based on *His purpose.*
And if He chose you, He intends to carry you.

Gideon needed constant reassurance. He questioned God. He asked for signs, *twice*.
And God, in His mercy, didn't shame him. He met him in his weakness.
He strengthened his hands. He sent the right people. He even gave Gideon a prophetic word from his enemies' camp to confirm his victory before the battle even began.

That's how tender God is with our fears.

You don't have to fake strength for God.
You don't have to pretend to be confident.
You just have to say *yes*.

Because your *yes* will unlock supernatural strength.
Your *yes* will make room for divine strategy.
Your *yes* will allow God to do what only He can do, work powerfully through your weakness.

So, if you're feeling small today, remember this:
Gideon defeated an entire army with just 300 men. Not because he was strong, but because God was with him.

God doesn't call the fearless. He calls the willing.
He doesn't wait for you to feel ready; He makes you ready as you go.

Journal Prompts:

1. What fears or insecurities do I need to surrender to God today?

2. What has God called me to that feels "too big" or "too soon"?

3. How has God shown up for me in past seasons when I felt unqualified?

Prayer:

God, You see more in me than I often see in myself. You call me brave when I feel afraid. You call me chosen when I feel unworthy. Help me to trust Your voice more than my own doubt. Remind me that I don't need to have all the answers to say yes. I don't have to be perfect to be used by You. Strengthen my heart when fear rises. Give me the courage to obey, even when I feel unqualified. Thank You for walking with me like You walked with Gideon patiently, powerfully, and faithfully. I believe that Your presence is my qualification. In Jesus' name, Amen.

Journal Notes:

Journal Notes:

Day 85:

Beauty for Ashes

Scripture:

"To bestow on them a crown of beauty instead of ashes, the oil of joy instead of mourning..."—Isaiah 61:3 (NIV)

Devotional Reflection:

Ashes are what remain after something has been burned.
They represent finality.
The end of what once was.
The residue of something that couldn't be salvaged.

You've likely stood in the middle of those ashes, watching the aftermath of dreams deferred, relationships dissolved, or seasons that didn't end with closure.
Ashes carry the weight of disappointment, loss, and grief.
They are messy. Uncomfortable. They cling to you long after the fire has gone out.

But here's the truth that shifts everything:
God doesn't leave us in the rubble. He meets us there, and then He redeems.

In Isaiah 61, He makes a holy promise: *to give you beauty instead of ashes.*
Not a surface-level beauty.
Not a fake smile or a bandaged wound.

But a beauty that rises *from* the ashes. A divine transformation that only He can do.

This is not cosmetic; it's spiritual.

God doesn't just decorate your ruins, He rebuilds them.
He doesn't just mend what's been broken, He reimagines it into something greater.

When your heart has been shattered, He shapes it into something softer and stronger.
When your plans have burned down, He reveals a new path forward, one that's Spirit-led, not self-made.

The ashes in your life are not wasted.
They are the very place God begins again.

Sometimes we fear letting go of what was because it's all we've known.
But holding on to ashes leaves no room for new life.
To receive beauty, you have to *release* what burned.
You have to lay the loss at His feet, not to forget it, but to let Him redeem it.

God is not intimidated by your wreckage.
He specializes in restoration.
He sees past what was lost and envisions what can still be found.
Where you see ruin, He sees the framework of something glorious.

And no, it won't always look the same.
It may not come packaged how you imagined.
But it will be full of Him, full of grace, healing, and purpose.

Your ashes are not your identity.
They are your testimony in the making.

Journal Prompts:

1. What are some "ashes" I've been holding onto that I need to surrender to God?

   ____
   ____
   ____

2. In what areas of my life do I need to believe again that God can bring beauty from pain?

   ____
   ____
   ____

3. How have I seen God rebuild something in the past that I thought was lost?

   ____
   ____
   ____

Prayer:

God, I come to You with the ashes of what was, of things that broke, dreams that died, and moments that didn't go the way I hoped. Some days, I feel like all I have left is pain. But I choose to believe that You are the God of divine exchange. You do not waste my sorrow. You do not overlook my grief. You promise beauty, not in spite of my ashes, but in exchange for them. So, I offer You every piece of what's burned, and I open my hands to receive what only You can give. Rebuild me. Restore me. Rewrite my story in Your timing and Your way. In Jesus' name, Amen.

Journal Notes:

Journal Notes:

Day 86:

The Wilderness Is a Womb

Scripture:

"Remember how the LORD your God led you all the way in the wilderness these forty years, to humble and test you in order to know what was in your heart, whether or not you would keep his commands. He humbled you, causing you to hunger and then feeding you with manna, which neither you nor your ancestors had known, to teach you that man does not live on bread alone but on every word that comes from the mouth of the LORD."—Deuteronomy 8:2-3 (NIV)

Devotional Reflection:

Wilderness seasons often feel like punishment, silent, dry, and desolate.
We assume God is distant when life gets quiet.
We panic when the familiar is stripped away.
We question our calling when fruit isn't visible.

But in God's hands, the wilderness becomes holy.

It's not the absence of purpose, it's the preparation for it.
It's not the rejection of who you are, it's the refinement of who you're becoming.

In Hosea 2:14, God says, *"I will allure her, and bring her into the wilderness, and speak tenderly to her."*

That doesn't sound like punishment. That sounds like pursuit.
God doesn't *push* you into the wilderness. He *draws* you there.
Because He knows that in the quiet, you will hear Him more clearly.
In the stripping, you will finally see what is essential.
In the stillness, He begins to rebuild you *from the inside out.*

The wilderness isn't a wasteland, it's a womb.
A place where the old is laid to rest and the new is quietly forming.
A place where you're no longer performing but being purified.
A place where God isn't punishing you, He's *preparing* you.

Look at Jesus. Before His public ministry began, He was led by the Spirit into the wilderness.
Not to prove Himself, but to be *anchored* in identity.
The wilderness affirmed who He was before He ever did a miracle.
And the same is true for you.

God doesn't just want to use you; He wants to *know* you.

So, if you find yourself in a place where the crowd is gone, the doors seem closed, or your direction feels unclear…
Pause and listen.
Because this might not be the enemy's attack.
It might be God's invitation.

Your wilderness is not where you're lost, it's where you're located.

And what feels like isolation is often divine insulation.
You're not being overlooked, you're being overshadowed by the presence of God.
You're not going backward, you're going deeper.

Don't despise this season.
Don't rush it.
Let it do its work in you.

When the time is right, the same God who led you in will lead you out with a clearer voice, a stronger heart, and a deeper intimacy that can never be shaken.

Journal Prompts:

1. In what ways have I misunderstood or resisted my wilderness season?

   ____
   ____
   ____
   ____
   ____
   ____

2. What distractions has God removed to help me hear Him more clearly?

   ____
   ____
   ____
   ____
   ____
   ____

3. What might God be birthing in me during this time of hiddenness?

   ____
   ____
   ____
   ____

Prayer:

God, thank You for meeting me in the wilderness. Even when I feel alone, Your presence is near. Help me not to run from the silence, but to lean into it, to hear what You're saying beneath the noise. Strip away every false comfort and fill me with the comfort of Your Spirit. Refine me in the hidden place. Remind me that I am not being punished, I am being prepared. Teach me to trust this season and to rest in the truth that You are doing a deeper work in me. I surrender my expectations and open my heart to what You're forming. In Jesus' name, Amen.

Journal Notes:

Journal Notes:

Day 87:

Faith Over Familiarity

Scripture:

"By faith Abraham...obeyed and went, even though he did not know where he was going."—Hebrews 11:8 (NIV)

Devotional Reflection:

Faith often asks you to leave what's familiar.
Not just places you've lived, but mindsets you've built.
Not just people you've walked with, but the roles you've hidden behind.
Not just jobs or titles, but identities shaped by survival, not surrender.

It's not just a move, it's a *release.*

Abraham didn't have a detailed plan. He didn't know where the road would take him.
He just had a word: *"Go."*
And that was enough, because the word came from the One who cannot lie.

Faith will stretch you.
It will challenge your logic, confront your comfort, and call you out of the shallow end.
It won't always feel secure, but it will always be sacred.

Sometimes what feels like "home" is actually a holding place for who you used to be.
Sometimes the most courageous thing you can do is admit: "I can't grow here anymore."

Letting go is holy.
Not everything you started with can come with you into your next season.
And that's not failure, that's formation.

You may be tempted to cling to what's predictable, what's proven, or what once worked.
But familiarity is not the same as fruitfulness.
Comfort can become a cage when God is calling you higher.

Faith is not about having it all figured out. It's about trusting the One who does.
It's choosing purpose over predictability.
It's walking with questions but refusing to walk in fear.
It's saying "yes" even when your hands are trembling, because your heart knows Who you're following.

You're not just walking away from something.
You're walking *into* something.

God is not calling you out to abandon you, He's calling you out to *establish* you.

There's provision on the path.
There's clarity on the journey.
There's blessing in obedience.

Even when the road is unfamiliar, the Shepherd is not.

Journal Prompts:

1. What familiar places, patterns, or relationships am I being called to release?

____
____
____
____
____
____

2. In what ways am I holding onto safety more than surrender?

____
____
____
____
____
____

3. What does it mean for me to walk in faith in this current season?

____
____
____
____
____
____

Prayer:

Lord, give me the courage to leave what's familiar when You call me forward. Help me not to settle in places that no longer serve the woman You are calling me to become. Even when I feel afraid, remind me that faith is choosing You over comfort. Show me what I need to let go of mindsets, habits, or people, that are keeping me stuck in a lesser version of myself. I trust You, even when I don't have all the answers. I trust that You are leading me with love, and where You are taking me is worth everything I've had to release. Strengthen my steps. Quiet my fears. And anchor me in Your promise. In Jesus' name, Amen.

Journal Notes:

Journal Notes:

Day 88:

Grace for the Gaps

Scripture:

"My grace is sufficient for you, for my power is made perfect in weakness."—2 Corinthians 12:9 (NIV)

Devotional Reflection:

There will be moments when your best doesn't feel like enough.
When you've prayed, planned, pushed and still feel like you're falling short.
When you're doing everything you can to stand, but the weight of "not enough" keeps pulling you down.
It's in those moments the enemy whispers lies:
"You're failing."
"You're not strong enough."
"You should be further along by now."

But God meets you right there.
Not in the illusion of perfection, but in the *truth* of your need.
Grace lives in the gaps.

God's grace is not a backup plan; it's the *only* plan.
It is divine strength for human limits.
It's the bridge between your insufficiency and God's infinite ability.

When Paul cried out for his weakness to be removed, God didn't change the circumstance.
He changed the perspective.
He said, *"My grace is sufficient for you, for My power is made perfect in weakness."*

God wasn't disappointed in Paul's need; He was drawn to it.

And He's drawn to yours too.

Your limitations are not a liability in the Kingdom, they're an invitation.
An invitation for God to step in and do what only He can.
To be glorified not *in spite* of your weakness, but *through* it.

You don't have to pretend to be strong all the time.
You don't have to carry what only God can sustain.
You don't have to be the answer, He already is.

When your best feels like it's falling short, remember:
God doesn't need your perfection, He desires your surrender.
He doesn't work around your weakness, He works through it.
And His grace never runs out.

Journal Prompts:

1. In what areas of my life do I feel like my best isn't enough?

   ____
   ____
   ____
   ____
   ____

____

2. How have I seen God's grace meet me in seasons of weakness?

____
____
____
____
____
____

3. What would it look like to release the pressure to be perfect and embrace dependence on God?

____
____
____
____
____
____

Prayer:

Father, thank You for reminding me that I don't have to carry it all. Thank You for meeting me in the middle of my mess, in the stretch between where I am and where I want to be. Help me to stop striving for perfection and start surrendering to Your presence. Remind me that Your grace isn't earned, it's given. When I feel like I'm not enough, remind me that You are more than enough. Fill my gaps with Your strength, cover my weaknesses with Your power, and let my life be a testimony to what You can do with someone fully dependent on You. I trust You with my limits and I welcome Your grace. In Jesus' name, Amen.

Journal Notes:

Day 89:

You're Not the Same Woman

Scripture:

"And I will give you a new heart, and a new spirit I will put within you. I will remove the heart of stone from your flesh and give you a heart of flesh." —Ezekiel 36:26 (ESV)

Devotional Reflection:

As you near the end of this journey, it's important to pause and acknowledge something powerful:

You are not the same woman who started this.
Yes, there may still be some healing ahead.
Yes, there may still be moments of uncertainty.
But do not let that make you overlook the sacred work that has already taken place within you.

You've grown in places no one can see.
You've surrendered battles only God knows about.
You've traded shame for grace, fear for faith, and silence for strength.
You may have started this journey searching but look at you now:
You are standing. You are healing. You are becoming.

God has been doing a new thing in you.
Not in loud, flashy ways, but in the quiet, hidden moments

where you chose obedience over comfort, presence over performance, and truth over denial.

Sometimes transformation doesn't look like fireworks, it looks like staying when you wanted to run, praying when you felt nothing, believing when it hurt, and trusting God through the unknown.

It looks like shedding old identities and embracing who you are in Christ, flawed, but favored. Broken, but being rebuilt. Growing, even when it felt like nothing was changing.

Look again:

- You've faced hard truths with courage.
- You've let go of people and patterns that no longer served your purpose.
- You've chosen healing over hiding, forgiveness over bitterness, progress over perfection.
- You've walked with God, not just when it was easy, but when it was dark, lonely, and quiet.

That is not small.
That is not ordinary.
That is *transformation.*

You didn't just survive, you evolved.
You didn't just wander, you were led.
And you didn't just find yourself; you rediscovered the God who never lost sight of you.

You can't go back to who you were, because she's no longer here.
And that's a *good* thing.

You are rising.
You are becoming.
You are ready for what's next.

God has called you forward, and what's ahead is greater, deeper, and more aligned with your purpose than anything you've left behind.

Journal Prompts:

1. How have I changed since the beginning of this journey, mentally, spiritually, emotionally?

   ____

   ____

   ____

   ____

   ____

   ____

2. What am I proud of myself for doing or letting go of?

   ____

   ____

   ____

   ____

   ____

   ____

3. What truth will I carry with me as I step into the next season?

   ____

   ____

   ____

   ____

Prayer:

God, thank You for walking with me every step of this journey. Thank You for the growth I didn't always see but now feel deep within me. I lay down who I was, and I receive who You've been shaping me to become. I may not have all the answers, but I have more of You and that's more than enough. Help me to move forward with courage, with clarity, and with confidence that You are still writing my story. I release the need to go back and embrace the beauty of becoming. Thank You for transforming me from the inside out. I give You all the glory. In Jesus' name, Amen.

Journal Notes:

Journal Notes:

Day 90:

The Journey Continues

Scripture:

"Being confident of this, that He who began a good work in you will carry it on to completion..."—Philippians 1:6 (NIV)

Devotional Reflection:

This may be Day 90, but it is not the end.
It's a threshold. A launching point.
The end of this devotional is not the end of your journey; it's the beginning of something greater than you could have imagined when you first started.

You began this solo journey with questions, wounds, and hopes tucked deep inside your heart.
You came seeking clarity, healing, and purpose.
And while you may not have received every answer, you've received something even more valuable: *alignment with your true identity in Christ.*

This journey was never just about discovery.
It was about *becoming.*
And becoming takes time, courage, and surrender.

You've:

- Peeled back layers that no longer served you.

- Reclaimed the truth of who you are.
- Surrendered pain that once silenced you.
- Made room for joy, for healing, for growth.
- Chosen wholeness over busyness and purpose over pressure.

But hear this:
There is more.
God is not done.

The good work He began in you is *still unfolding.*
Even now, He is preparing your next steps, opening new doors, and making ways in the wilderness.
Every brave decision you make from here, every "yes," every "no," every boundary, every prayer, is another brick in the foundation of the life He's building through you.

This isn't the end. It's the becoming.
There will be new lessons that deepen your wisdom.
New healing that frees your heart.
New opportunities that require your bold obedience.

And you'll be ready because of what you've learned, what you've laid down, and what you've embraced in this sacred space.

God doesn't waste anything, not your pain, not your silence, not even your detours.
He's the Master Builder, and He never leaves work undone.
What He started in you, He will complete (Philippians 1:6).

So let this final page be a *marker,* not a period.
A moment to pause, celebrate, and commit, not to perfection, but to persistence.

Go back and reread your reflections.
Revisit the prayers you wept through.
Remember how far you've come, and how faithful God has been.

And when doubt tries to whisper that you're still alone, remind yourself of this truth:

You were never alone.
Not on Day 1.
Not on Day 47.
Not now. Not ever.

God walked with you then.
He walks with you now.
And He will walk with you into *whatever comes next.*

You are not finished;
You are *becoming.*

Journal Prompts:

1. What do I know about myself that I didn't fully believe before?

____
____
____
____
____
____

2. What do I want to carry with me into this next chapter?

____
____
____
____
____
____

3. How can I stay grounded in the truth of who I am when life gets loud again?

____
____
____
____
____
____

Prayer:

God, thank You for every page, every tear, every breakthrough, and every whisper of grace along this journey. Thank You for never leaving me, even when I felt lost. I give You glory for the healing You've begun, the strength You've built in me, and the identity You've reaffirmed. I know this isn't the end, it's just the beginning of a greater becoming. Help me to walk boldly in the truth of who I am and whose I am. Remind me daily that I'm not walking alone. I trust You to finish the work You started and to lead me into a future full of purpose, healing, and light. In Jesus' name, Amen.

Journal Notes:

Journal Notes:

About the Author

Dr. Rita Carter is the Founder and CEO of Breakthrough, a global organization dedicated to helping women live authentically, walk boldly in their purpose, and create thriving relationships. A certified transformation coach, best-selling author, and captivating speaker, Dr. Rita has devoted over two decades to empowering others to break through barriers and step into the fullness of who God created them to be.

With a rich background in leadership, emotional intelligence, and personal development, Dr. Rita brings both professional expertise and Spirit-led wisdom to her work. She is also a certified DISC Consultant, equipping individuals and organizations to better understand themselves and others in order to build stronger, healthier connections.

Known for her compassionate, practical, and faith-centered approach, Dr. Rita creates safe spaces where women can heal, grow, and rise. She blends biblical truth with relatable storytelling, guiding others to release what no longer serves them and embrace the freedom found in Christ.

When she's not coaching, speaking, or writing, Dr. Rita treasures her time with family in Michigan. Her greatest joy is seeing women embrace their authentic selves and walk courageously into their God-given destiny.

Solo Journey is more than a devotional; it is Dr. Rita's heart poured onto the page, an invitation for every woman to discover that she is never truly walking alone.

Connect With Me

To learn more about Dr. Rita's coaching and speaking services or to schedule a free discovery call, please visit her website at
www.breakthroughready.com

Social Media:

Facebook:
https://www.facebook.com/BreakthroughwithRita
Instagram: https://www.instagram.com/breakthroughwithrita/

www.ingramcontent.com/pod-product-compliance
Lightning Source LLC
Chambersburg PA
CBHW040512170726
48295CB00012B/175
9781955107266